VISION AND SPIRIT

An Essay on Plato's Warrior Class

Joe Simmons

UNIVERSITY
PRESS OF
AMERICA

Lanham • New York • London

Copyright © 1988 by

University Press of America,® Inc.

4720 Boston Way
Lanham, MD 20706

3 Henrietta Street
London WC2E 8LU England

Printed in the United States of America

British Cataloging in Publication Information Available

Library of Congress Cataloging-in-Publication Data

Simmons, Joe.
Vision and spirit : an essay on Plato's warrior class / Joe
Simmons.
p. cm.
Bibliography: p.
1. Soldiers—Conduct of life. 2. War—Moral and ethical aspects.
3. War—Religious aspects. 4. Plato. Republic. I. Title.
U22.S54   1988
174'.9355—dc 19   88–1401 CIP
ISBN 0–8191–6885–8 (alk. paper)
ISBN 0–8191–6886–6 (pbk. : alk. paper)

All University Press of America books are produced on acid-free
paper which exceeds the minimum standards set by the National
Historical Publications and Records Commission.

This book is dedicated to my father, Hugh Michael Simmons, who taught me to love the life of self-forgetful action, and to my mother, Katherine Agnes Simmons, who taught me to love the life of contemplation.

"Bad men rule by the feebleness of the ruled if they allow the wicked to defeat them. It is precisely because they themselves are evil in certain respects. (Those who) from softness and indolence let the wolves tear them to pieces like fatted lambs (will not be victorious). Not even a god will defend unwarlike men. The divine law decrees that those who fight bravely should be rescued from battle, not those who (simply) pray."

Plotinus

"Desire upon desire for the highest so came to me that at every step I felt my wings grow for the flight."

Dante

"The most royal of kings is he who is king over himself."

Plato

PREFACE

I wish to thank the Educational Foundation in India for the Fulbright Scholarship that allowed me to study Indian literature in India during the summer of 1986. I am indebted to those who helped me in the manuscript preparation while I was occupied with chairing both the philosophy department and our college honors program. Their help was inestimable during this very busy year. I also wish to thank the Los Rios College Board for their grant of partial release time for the development of our new honors classes. It was in preparation for our first honors class in classical Greek thought that I was able, once more, to seriously delve into Plato's ideas.

INTRODUCTION

Few single books have been written about Plato's warrior class. This may be because his ideas on the subject are scattered in a brief and random fashion throughout his writings. They never seem central to the goals of his conversations. However, I believe that his ideas on the subject shed light on the whole conception of the Platonic quest for a unifying vision. Much that Plato says would seem to indicate that the vision which he conveys is itself the transformational agent of human nature. Vision makes spirit. I believe that this view can be modified by exploring Plato's development of a philosophic class by military training. For Plato it is the intellectual and moral discipline for war which makes a spirit susceptible to vision. If this is so then character precedes knowledge. I also believe that much can be gleaned on this subject from neo-Platonic influences long after Plato's academy ceased to exist. In the development of the warrior code, neo-Platonic thought may be truer to Plato than in any other respect. I also would like to suggest that we can understand the atmosphere of Plato's ideas about the warrior ethos by looking at the pre-Platonic thought of Homer.

By gathering these scattered fragments of pre-Plato and post-Plato and reuniting them in accordance with the Platonic texts, we may be able to round out the brief vision Plato gives about the nature of the warrior ethos. In this task I wish to be a very small mediator of very great ideas.

For Plato, the warrior ethos is central for the path of the spirit. His military class is a class of high social status, as well as a preparation for the mystic vision. Military training is essentially ethical. It is this warrior ethos, this discipline in virtue, which gives the military class its nature. In Plato's vision of the military profession, there is a combination of the philosophic and religious vocation applied directly to war. Like the Zen component in the samurai tradition, or the Judeo-Christian component in the code of knighthood, Plato's religious views permeate his military concepts.

These Platonic concepts are timeless. In our day and age, so far in many respects from the times of Plato, we need to once again ponder on the notions of the warrior ethos. The code of knighthood, be it grounded in the path of the Dorian warrior, the way of the medieval chevalier, or the training of a member of the American special forces, is as necessary today as it ever was.

In Plato's thought, however, there is a further application for the discipline of military training. The very same traits of character needed for the men and women in his Greek military companies are the same traits of character needed for the path of philosophy and life itself. War, before it is externalized on the battlefield, is internalized in the individual soul. In the _Republic_, Plato does much more than set out a political philosophy. He describes the male and female soldiers molded on his archetypical warrior pattern. He describes the relationship between the sexes. He ends his account with the myth of Er and a final judgment. A book that opens with the Socratic worship of a local goddess, and a discussion of sex and death, and ends with a vision of ultimate moral accountability is more than a book on politics.

For us, today, his concepts of wisdom, justice, courage, and temperance, all essential elements of a warrior ethos, are a necessary renaissance of forgotten necessities lost in a haze of technology and indifference. The woman alone on the streets at night, the law enforcement officer, the fire fighter, or the military professional all must live by the warrior ethos. Above all, the spiritual path, with its resolution of moral warfare, is rooted in the notions of Plato's silver knights.

It is in this respect that the warrior Ethos is central to all human existence, civilian or military alike. Above all, Plato believes it is essential for the path of philosophy. Nothing separates Plato further from the modern classrooms of contemporary education, not even his views on democracy or platonic love, than his emphasis on the warrior code as a way to knowledge and its consequent self-sacrificing action. For Plato not only does vision make spirit, but spirit in its most martial form makes vision.

Since it was not central to my main task, I have placed a discussion of Plato's religious insight in Appendix I. I have also included some material on the Zen military tradition in Japan and some excerpts from J.R.R. Tolkein from my first book, The Warrior, Studies in Sport, War, and Spiritual Mastery. (University Press of America, 1982)

I will attempt to do three things: (1.) To look at the components of Greek thought which, in a general way, contribute to Plato's warrior ethos. (2.) To look at what Plato said about the nature of the warrior class. (3.) To compare briefly these ideas with Indian, Japanese, medieval, and Homeric thought. In doing these three things, I hope to develop a small, beginning mosaic, a picture of a warrior ethos, which is meant for ordinary life as well as war. I will point out that Plato's personal development in training for war is meant to be the essential preparation for the life of philosophy. This book is meant to be an introduction for those who are knowledgeable and intelligent but may not have a formal background in philosophy.

What picture comes to mind when we talk of a warrior par excellence? For most of us, the picture would fit the Byzantine Princess Anna Commena's description of Bohemund, llth Century crusader and Norman adventurer. Ambitious, pugnatious, and war-like, he was filled with contempt for death or fear. "There was not," she says, "a barbarian or Hellene who could measure up to him." This "Latin" Knight was "a marvel to behold." In her young eyes, horrified yet fascinated, "he was a legendary figure whose mere description took your breath away." There was a "mighty spirit boiling up from his heart." Though she found,"something attractive about the man's countenance," his" intimidating impression" conveyed the "mercilessness of a beast of prey." Physical and spiritual "ferocity and lust were always rampant in him." The primal forces expressed by his "heroic nostrils" were so much pent up passion" perpetually seeking vent in war." It was Norman barons, -like this crusader, who were the spearhead of the military offensive of the "Barbarian Latin West" in a new found aggressiveness against the more ancient and stable Byzantine East, as well as the military might of Islam. Were these successes in the fortunes of war founded on the elemental fury of a Bohemund?

Anna Commena' s picture of a man filled with the warrior ethos of convention may tell only half the tale. Unlike the Normans, such barbarian heros have little lasting military success. Her intelligent and observant young eyes may have missed in the Norman knight, if not in Bohemund, the spiritual center which radiated unparalled military success. The Latin West had itself surprisingly defeated the Scandinavian North, and the Magyar barbarian East, as well as the Islamic military on the Iberian Peninsula. As Toynbee points out, the West was a "civilization in a state of growth." Its moral center, its "spiritual citadel,"was the monastic rejuvenation of the Benedictine spiritual life, the "archetype" of all reforms "religious and secular." It was the Normans who were the most recent converts to this spiritual ascendancy. It was those very Normans who were the military advanced guard of the Western tradition. As Toynbee says, the Norman minstrel Taillefer, at the Battle of Hastings, did not sing a Norse Volsungasaga but the Song of Roland in French. It was these Norman converts to the Latin religion which spread Western military power in Apulia, Calabria, Sicily, and Constantinople. And it is arguable that it was the Norman society that was the most religious of the Western cultures.

I will argue that it is one's spiritual vision that is a most important component of any warrior ethos. Savageness and fearlessness are themselves useless without an ethos that is grounded in spiritual vision. I want to reintroduce into contemporary discussions about the warrior ethos (small enough in the late 20th century), the ideas of Plato. For Plato, military smartness deals with the properties of our souls its destiny and its moral nature. In an age of the technician and the sophistication of the instruments of war or training systems based on cruelty and fury for their own sake, we need to again ponder the Platonic notions of developing a warrior class.

I will be happy if I can once again focus discussion on the connection between the vocations of the spirit and the path of the warrior. It may be that our Bohemunds and our St.Benedicts are much closer than we might think. If this is so I believe that the connection may be found in the pre-Christian Greek thought of a Plato and it's historic extensions in Western culture. It is a picture that will not substitute intellectual refinement for moral discipline nor the training of the head at the expense of the soul, heart, and body.

The Greek word "askesis" means "exercise." When applied to body, mind, and spirit askesis becomes an ascetical discipline for the adept in Greek philosophy. In Plato the mind is exercised by dialectic in preparation for the vision of the Good. Socratic dialectic, when used by an artful master of the insightful question, liberates the memory for philosophic discipline. The soul would be exercised by moral training[1]. For Plato, to know virtue was to become virtuous. The mysteries of the divine ideals were to become the visionary ground of ethical action in human community. Finally, the body would be exercised by athletic training for sport and war. For Plato, the "gymnastic" exercise was a preparation for gnosis, for vision, and for the development of the soul. The golden order of sages in Plato's Republic were first trained in the silver order of warriors in preparation for philosophic wisdom. This book will explore the conceptual nature of this novel idea.

What does the Greek mind see in the moral and athletic training of a professional military class that would be necessary for the path of philosophic enlightenment? To answer this question I will look at Plato's ideas as expressed in his writings. I will compare Plato's Greek philosophy with similar concepts in Indian, Chinese, and Japanese thought. I will also compare some notions of Plato with chivalric ideals in Europe during the Middle Ages. Sometimes there will be a parallel, sometimes a correspondence, and sometimes a contrast.

When Plato's friends were unclear about his philosophic meanings, Plato would use the language of story and myth to help conceptualize his ideas. I will follow his example, using literary examples from, among others, English novelists like J.R.R. Tolkein, C.S. Lewis, and Charles Williams. I think this is appropriate since their fiction is Platonic through and through.

Above all, I am interested in the most unusually philosophical development in western history. Because of its uniqueness, it is surprising so little has been said about it. For Plato the ideal philosopher is developed in a Greek military community. What are the elements of this military sisterhood and brotherhood which would develop the philosophical initiate into a metaphysical visionary?

In the Republic Plato divides society into three classes. The lowest class would include all trades and professions. It would include all economic classes and vocations from the poor to the wealthy. The second class is a warrior class. It would be composed of all professional military personnel. The highest class would be the class of philosophers, or guardians. Each class has a special symbol. The lowest class is "bronze" or "iron." The warrior class is "silver" and the highest class is "gold." Each class has a special virtue. The lowest class has the virtue of temperance. The warrior class has the virtue of courage. The highest class has the virtue of wisdom.

All members of society could volunteer for a testing process at age twenty. Criteria for advancement would be based on mental, moral, and physical excellence. The top group would then be trained for ten years. At this stage the warrior class (the "auxiliaries") and the guardians would be given the same Platonic development in ethics, mathematics, science, and athletics. At the age of thirty this group would be tested again. At that time the creme de la creme would become guardians. This golden order of philosophers would continue studying Platonic philosophy for five more years. At the age of thirty-five they would return to the lowest class for fifteen years, mixing with the general populace which they eventually rule. At age fifty the guardians would take office as the philosophical and political elite of Plato's ideal society.

The silver order of warriors and the golden order of philosophers would be celibate and own no property. Like a medieval military brotherhood they would take vows of poverty and chastity. (For some, there would be brief exceptions to the vow of chastity. Selected members might be allowed to produce children by command of the parliament of guardians.) Both elite classes would continue to undergo athletic training. Both classes would be trained toward a vision of Plato's divine ideal world. The guardians would be trained for the philosophic vision of the Good ("agathon"), the highest divine knowledge possible. The warrior class would also have an elevated, though derivative, knowledge of this mystic vision.

Why does Plato want his most philosophic class trained as military professionals for ten years? Why does Plato want both of his elite classes to live without wealth? Why does Plato stress chastity as a prerequisite for membership in the orders of silver and gold? Why does Plato stress athletic training for both elite classes? Do these ideas have any meaning in the contemporary world?

The Republic is usually treated as a book on political philosophy. However, a book which opens up with a discussion on sex and death and ends with a story of the last judgment deals with more than political thought. It is permeated throughout with Plato's religious notions and his emphasis on athletic and military training. Socrates, at the very start of the dialogue, is about to "pray to the Goddess" Bendis (Rep. 327A).

Cephalus, facing death, is supremely happy that he is free from the "cruel and raging tyrant" (sex, drink, and parties) (Rep. 328A and 329C). Socrates is delighted (Rep. 329E). The Republic ends with admonitions about how to live without defiling our immortal souls, friendship with the gods, and "the upward path and practice of justice" (Rep. 621C).

* * * * *

Plato's concept of the training of the elite classes rests on his concept of mystic vision. The athletic and military training creates a climate for an ongoing knowledge and preparation for the vision of the Good (Rep. 509 A-C). It is a religious and spiritual understanding of the cosmic order. His warrior class, the auxiliaries (including the potential guardian class) are knights with a growing transcendental vision of Plato's mystic knowledge, and its consequent development of ideal character. It is in this sense that we might speak of Plato's warrior as a "cosmic knight," one whose military profession and power comes out of a "cosmic" vision of divine ideals. We may be able to understand Plato's emphasis on sport, refined monasticism, and vision by looking more closely at the connection between these disparate activities.[2]

If the training of Plato's most philosophical class is best done by ten years of training in his order of cosmic knights, would it follow that the best training for a warrior class would be ethical, philosophical, and visionary? Plato thought there was reciprocity between the two vocations. Do his ideas have any value for the twentieth century and the perennial quest for self-development?

In Plato we have the Greek legacy at its highest. In the <u>Republic</u> Plato expresses a vision of an ideal community, one that allows the full development of the self. He is not interested in the development of happiness in the ordinary sense, but of "justice" (dikaiosune). This <u>dikaiosune</u>, however, is not essentially social or political. The Greek concept of dikaiosune is closer to the notion of respiritualizing the self. In Latin the word "ligare" means to bind together, to unite. "Religion" means to re-bind that which is disunited, to "re-ligare" the fragmented spirit. Dikaiosune, for Plato, is more of a concept of soul rightness than of social law. It is "religious" in its core.

For Plato, philosophy can develop one's "logistikon," or reasoning ability. This is a preparation for the emancipation of the "nous" by which the philosopher gains spiritual insight into the ideal vision of reality.[3]

To know "eide," the archetypical essences of things, is to be the true philosopher, the guardian of the ideas. It is to have the pure vision (noesis) of the wise. For Plato this knowledge is an "anamnesis," a remembrance of that which we once knew but have forgotten through some moral fault.[4]

Because it is a moral fault which has caused our loss of the ideals it must be by moral training that the self returns, is re-bound, re-spiritualized, for its ascent toward wisdom.[5] For a classical Greek like Plato it is the quest for the balanced spirit (sophrosyne) which is the philosophical path for the wayfarer. It is sophrosyne, the re-integration of the parts of the soul, which gives the philosopher the temperament for knowledge. This temperament is a character at once bold and humble.[6] The soul must be filled with "arete," a moral excellence endowed with self-control.

The lowest part of the soul, filled with the desires and cravings for pleasure (epithumia) must give way to the higher passion, the spirited nature (thumos) which is used in war. All of these powers must be guided by reason (logistikon), itself filled with the vision of the <u>Good</u> (agathon). The philosophic way must be a "katharsis" (purification), a study in temperance and discipline of mind, body, and soul (psyche). This discipline produces "harmonia" (balance) and integrates the scattered pieces of the self into its original unity. The philosopher on this path is like a Pythagorian initiate, since the purification of the soul must involve the total self. It is only then that one sees the summum bonum of the <u>quest</u>, goodness in all of its splendor.

Plato perpetuates the Greek ideal of athletics as one means of this philosophic discipline. For the Greeks it was the gymnasium and the palaistrai (place of physical culture) which were the training grounds for citizenship in Greek culture. From thirteen to nineteen the youth were trained in boxing, wrestling, running, jumping, spear-throwing, and the tossing of the discus. Skill, beauty, and strength were all rounded out by military training at nineteen. For Plato this would be combined with philosophy and poetry in a study that was in the fullest sense a sacred humanism.

In his ideal republic Plato does all of this in the warrior class, the auxiliaries. It was in the training for sport and war that the Platonic esoterici were prepared for philosophic vision. It was military preparation which was to make the individual "just," to create the tone for "spirit," to make dikaiosune a reality in the inner life of the warrior-guardian.[7]

Plato's psychology of the soul may correspond not only to the Indian concepts of tamas, rajas, and sattva (sensual feeling, martial spirit, and rationality), but to Plato's three political classes. The class of bronze (the merchant-prince) has the nature of epithumia. Therefore, the chief virtue needed is temperance. The class of silver (the warrior) has the nature of thumos. Therefore, its chief virtue is courage or martial valor. The class of gold (the sage) has the nature of logistikon. Therefore, its chief virtue is wisdom, or spiritual insight. It is tempting to see in all of this, not a description of political and social institutions, but a description of the ideal Greek self. The men and women who truly have the purified, balanced, moral excellence of "justice" would be a harmonious balance of all three orders. It is the class of silver, the order of warriors, which is the mean point or the balancing connection between the lower and higher orders. This idea would not negate the existential reality of differing proportions of the ideal in different people.

Though martial courage would not be the most important virtue for the merchant-prince, it would be present in some important degree for his perfection as an individual. Though the vision of the Good in its fullest form would not be necessary for the military class, it would be, according to Plato, a guiding concept in a derivative way, just as the bronze temperance would be assumed in the silver class. The sage or guardian would also combine all virtues subsumed under the mystic knowledge of the Good.

In short, Plato's doctrine of the powers of the soul, the vocations in the social order, and the goal of philosophical inquiry correspond to a training system, a humanism grounded in spiritual knowledge, which would be best achieved in the self-development of the military order of his Greek silver knights. His means are unique in western thought. The goal is a genuine liberation of the human spirit for ascendance toward the divine by training the potential philosopher for the clash of phalanxes on the battlefields of Asia Minor and the eastern Mediterranean.

Plato's two elite classes studied the ultimate forms: beauty, goodness, justice, temperance, and knowledge. The philosopher or guardian, an end product of athletic and military training, was not simply to be a knower of truths but a lover of these truths. The "lover of honor," if he cannot be a commander, will "serve as a lieutenant" (Rep. 475a). The true philosopher will be a "lover of wisdom" (Rep. 475e). The attitude and temperament of the one, the warrior, is a preparation for the attitude and temperament of the other, the philosopher. In the Symposium and the Phaedrus, beauty is, in Gregory Vlastos' words, "the lure for love." This appetite for love "voracious but omnivorous" starts with physical forms and ascends to the beatific vision of all desire (Symp. 210e).

For Plato, this quest for knowledge is a quest for character, for the development of the self. The honor-loving warrior is not only superior to the man of business (Rep. 583a) but has the possibility of attaining true guardianship, an ultimate knowledge of reality which leads to a transcendent detachment from the slips of fortune (Rep. 586e). The soul of the knower is one's own.

It is in the vision of the elite forms which are orderly and constant that the philosopher "will himself become as harmonious and divine as any man may be" (Rep. 500c-d). Here Plato touches on a mystic dimension in his thinking. This philosophic knowledge or vision is a "celebration of perfect mysteries" (Phaed. 249c). The initiate who is God-possessed, one with God, is one who "philosophized rightly" (Phaed. 69c-d). In Vlastos' words, the Platonic philosopher finds "happiness, beauty, knowledge, moral sustenance, and regeneration. . .a mystical sense of this kinship with eternal perfection." Platonism is a novel metaphysics founded on mystical apprehension. The Platonic philosopher is the hero who lives in time while increasing his vision of eternity. This aptitude for a double vision of two dimensions at once is the process of ten years of training in Plato's military class. For Plato, training in a professional Greek military order was the best preparation for the mystic quest which goes beyond the ontological language of philosophy. The elite military society of the ideal republic was the seminal training ground for the hard-eyed mystics of mathematics, science, metaphysical, and transcendental forms which alone gave meaning and value to the Platonic view of human existence. It was here that grace and poise would come out of a holy fraternity.

* * * * *

In his novel <u>Lord of The Rings</u>, J.R.R. Tolkien draws a portrait of great splendor. It is a picture of a world falling into darkness. The powers of evil are on the move, fanning out through the lands of light and innocence.

The Black Riders hunt, sniffing the earth, looking for the one ring of power which would seal the fate of the universe. The evil and powerful magician Sauron, merciless and greedy, marshals his trained legions of darkness, his hideous Orcs, to conquer the world.

Between him and the control of the earth there are the weak and innocent Hobbits. They are simple and untrained. It is a time in which the West needs warriors to fight back against the encroaching flood of power, skill, and numbers in the service of Mordor, the kingdom of tyranny and evil. Unfortunately for the West, their warriors are few and far between. The kingdoms of freedom and light are on the defensive and have lost their spiritual might. The momentum has swung toward Sauron and his hosts of evil. In the midst of the universal conflagration about to sweep across Middle Earth, however, there are a few warriors who aid and train the little Hobbits for the task of ring bearers.

Among these few is Glorfindel, the elf-warrior. Transcendental, courageous and knightly, he is the model of a perfect warrior in any age. Glorfindel's military might comes from his spiritual nature; his mind is in two places at once. It is focused on the heavenly kingdom of light. It is here that he draws his strength for the essential task at hand. It is his unpleasant duty to stand for the decaying power of the West against the overwhelming power of Mordor. His mind must move from the brilliant fire of the divine realm to the earthly war of pain, dirt, blood, and death. In short, he must function on two planes at once.

As a warrior, he must be a competent swordsman, archer, and horseman. His technical skill must be brought to perfection to meet the skill of the aggressors of Sauron. His power works through, but does not come from, mind and muscle. He rides as one skilled in the arts of war and spirit to face the Black Riders trained only in the art of war.

In the colorful portrayal of Glorfindel, the elflord, Tolkien has drawn a sketch of great beauty and power. In Glorfindel, the kingdoms of earth and heaven unite to produce an image of high courage and nobility.

Glorfindel is a Cosmic Knight. The moral claims of the universe, seen with the ethical insight of a mystic, are the basis of his heroic actions when war is inevitable. At worst they can be defeated but never disgraced. At best they will become lords of might and power.

* * * * *

In classical Japan, archery became a means of self-mastery and spiritual development. A western philosopher, Eugen Herrigel, underwent such training with the guidance of a master archer and Zen master. It was a long and disciplined system of training, and Herrigel left an interesting account of his moral, mental, and emotional enrichment in a small book called Zen in the Art of Archery.

The contest, Herrigel discovered, is really with the archer himself. It is, in fact, the foundation of all contests that seem outwardly directed. In the spiritual Zen tradition of Japan, ink painting, tea ceremonies, flower arrangement, swordsmanship, martial arts, and archery become the means of enlightenment. The Zen disciple was nurtured in an ancient tradition which had been refined and tested over many centuries. He would learn the importance of breath control, the difficult task of physical spontaneity, and relaxation in movement and action. These technical aspects of the art of archery will be drilled into the aspiring student with a seemingly endless non-western patience and demanding discipline. Always present, however, is the demonstration and example of the Zen master, modeling the appropriate way of the spirit, demanding excellence, developing intuition in the eager but clumsy disciple. The master of any craft, he soon learns, must become a competent artisan before he can become an artist. Only then, Herrigel was taught, will the mastery of form no longer oppress, but liberate.

In learning to shoot the long-bow of the ancient Samurai, the student of Zen spirituality must develop concentration and self-forgetfulness. The mind must become flexible, nimble, and spiritual. In fact, there comes a danger point when the student becomes quite successful at the technique of archery. Praise for military and athletic power threatens to freeze him as an artisan instead of an artist. As if it were hardly worth a mention, the master points out that right action is only accomplished in a state of selflessness. In success he was to be as tranquil as in defeat.

He was not to grieve over bad shots or become unusually proud over good ones. He was to be free from the buffetings of pleasure and pain. He was only to rejoice in the mysterious "other" who shot well. An ancient military discipline had to become a vehicle of spiritual development. The target had to become the untrained human nature, willful and disobedient. Archery had to become the medium of moral refinement.

In the military manual of Takuan, the collective wisdom of the Japanese swordmasters expressed this concept. They knew that however strong, pugnacious, courageous, or fearless one is he must enter into the discipline of spiritual training where his confidence in his strong body and mind must be eroded. His confidence must be placed in the mysterious "other." Like any athlete or warrior, the young student on the path of the Bushido, the life of a Samurai, must realize that he is at the mercy of the stronger, the more athletic, the more cunning, or the chance circumstance of a general battle. On any day he can be defeated.

He must learn smooth, flowing, response where his "psyche" is disciplined in a focus of active relaxation. The spontaneity allows the "other" to perform in a long process of unexampled discipline. The archer must become quiet, unassuming, nonchalant without the least desire to show off. The Zen tradition emphasized rigorous and protracted training for self-conquest. The hall in which Japanese fencing is conducted is called the hall of enlightenment.

* * * * *

Plato's ideal community is a type of military academy for the development of elite classes of silver and gold. Plato's golden sages are sagacious without ceasing to be silver warriors. Here the Samurai tradition in Japan is paralleled in the west by Plato's ideal republic and its emphasis on a communal development of the Greek military professional. Sport for Plato is a means of moral development just as it is in the Zen tradition.

In his Aspasia, Aeschines says Socrates believed that the goodness of women was "the same as that of a man."[8] In the Republic, after a discussion on women, Socrates says that "we still haven't been shown that a woman differs from a man in what we have been talking about," i.e., membership in the warrior-guardian class (Rep. 454e). These women, "since they wear excellence in place of clothes" must "be partners in warfare" (Rep. 457a). He adds that their tasks "will be lighter," probably because of the female body being smaller (Rep. 457b). The "guardians and guardiennes," however, "will pursue everything in common" (Rep. 457c). The women warriors in the Republic were probably modeled after Aspasia and Rhodogyne.[9] Since these women will exercise naked (Rep. 457b) it is also hard to avoid the influence of Sparta on Plato's thought. In the Laws Plato had argued that from the age of six both sexes will be taught how to ride and fight with bow, sling, spear and shield (Laws 794c-d). He wants both male and female to have "two right hands" i.e., be ambidextrous. Here the gymnastics would include dancing in armor and wrestling (Laws 796 b-d). These competitions, the Athenian says, are "beneficial alike to the community and the individual household" (Laws 796d). Even the expectant mother must exercise for the child's sake (Laws 789d).

The ideal of the warrior-guardian community for Plato is a mix of intelligent, athletic, Greek males and females.

In Sparta the males began training for war around the age of six. Women and men practiced sport, including boxing and wrestling, in the nude. At sixteen the young women of Sparta marched in a nude parade.

This was to encourage them to work out hard and stay in shape. Spartan women were famous for their physical beauty and martial ardor. (As the men marched off to war they would chant "come home with your shield or on it.") Plato would want to incorporate these types of women in his ideal orders of gold and silver while at the same time making due allowances for differing natures (Rep. 457a), especially in childbirth (Rep. 461a).

8

There is a parallel here between Greek and Indian thought. Indian dynamic yoga is a preparation for insight and a liturgical form of religious worship. One type of gymnastic movement is called surya pranam. It is a ten stage movement involving all the major muscle groups of the body. When done with speed and concentration it is highly aerobic and develops great flexibility. However, that is not why Indian yogans do the exercise. "Surya" is derived from the root "su" meaning "creation." "Surya" is another name for the creator or supreme Hindu divinity. From the divinity comes "prakriti" or dynamic creative energy. In ancient India the sun was both a symbol and materialistic source for this creative heat and light.[10]

This gymnastic movement, or "sun prayers" was performed as a disciplined athletic yoga, affecting mind, body, and spirit. Here the purpose for Indian dynamic yoga would be the same as Plato's basic gymnastic training. Athletics became "religious" training. Exercise had become ritual.

For Plato, the ascent towards spiritual vision and fulfillment begins with our organic nature. The philosopher and mystic visionary begins as an athlete. The organic nature is disciplined as a means of developing one's soul. In the Republic Socrates perpetuates the Greek concept of a sound mind in a sound body through athletic training. (Plato himself was a competitive wrestler in the Greek Olympic Games. "Platon" is a nickname meaning "broad shouldered, well muscled, and large.")

For Plato exercise and sport is ascetical. It develops "askesis," the ability to discipline oneself in preparation for action. Running, wrestling, boxing, and weight training for war were part of the Greek cultural fabric. Sport was a preparation for war.

In Sparta vertical jumps were used for conditioning. Many Spartan women could do these vertical jumps by the hundreds. Again, the exercises used by Plato would be of like nature to these Indian and Spartan gymnastic movements. Plato based the beginning steps of spiritual mastery on these types of gymnastic dancing. Though we do not know all the specifics of his athletic programs, we do know from the Republic the great importance Plato attaches to these athletic exercises. Why, we may ask, does Plato treat this Greek "yoga" with such reverence? Plato's teacher Socrates had drawn from Greek culture his notions about sport. For classical Greece there was an intrinsic connection between sport and character. ("Gymnastics" for Plato meant exercise in general though he refers to some specific athletic movements throughout his writings.)

It is at this point that Plato gives an interesting twist to his concept of the reciprocity between ritual exercise and self-development. In the Republic, Socrates says that "the excellence of a good body doesn't make the soul good" (Rep. 403d). It is the other way around. It is "the excellence of a good soul" which "makes the body as good as it can." He had already insisted that "after poetry the young must be trained in gymnastics." The youth must be an athlete, "carefully trained all through life from childhood up." If this "gymnastic" or physical training in general does not affect the soul (the spiritual and philosophic powers), why Plato's insistence on exercise? The answer, I believe, lies in line 404b. Here Socrates says that the "military athletes" need an athletic program which is "a sister" to "simple poetry." In line 404e he says that this "simplicity" will put "temperance in the soul" and "health in the body." In other words, Plato's warrior

9

class doesn't use physical training for bodily development, but for the development of the warrior/guardian's soul. Physical excellence is a by-product.

*****

Plato and Shankara essentially share the same vision of ultimate knowledge.[11] The spiritual path of Shankara is paralleled in Plato's allegory of the cave. In the Republic (Rep. 509c) "the Good" is described as "not being, but beyond being, surpassing it in dignity and power." The Good is the "cause of knowledge and truth." It gives "knowers the power to know." This Good is the means of and the goal of all philosophic vision. In the Republic Book 7, Rep. (514a) Socrates metaphorically describes the acquisition of gnosis as a journey from the darkness of a cave to the knowledge of reality in the daylight. In the cave, people are in chains. They literally have tunnel vision and can only see the shadows of things. This would correspond to the philosophic Indian beginner in the stage of "saravana." Through a "natural happening" one individual is released from his chains. It happens "suddenly." He is "forced to stand up." It causes him pain and blindness. This, however, is not a visionary experience, since he has not seen the sunlight but only the firelight in the cave. (This firelight, of course, is a fragment of true knowledge in the cave, that corresponds to the sunlight outside the cave.) Socrates supposes that someone "forcibly dragged him out of there." He is forced to journey "up that steep, rugged incline." This would correspond to the yogic stage of gradual awakening in manana.

Outside of the cave the initiate sees "the heavenly bodies and heaven itself." This takes place at night. Here is the full philosophic state of Shankara's manana. Finally the maturing visionary sees the sun, "the giver of seasons" (Rep. 516c). The "shape of the Good" is finally and with difficulty seen "in all of its glory" (Rep. 517c). It begets in the visible world "the Lord of light itself, the Lord-giver of truth and intelligence." This would correspond to the final Jnana yogic state of hididhy yasana, or habitual mental awareness of spiritual truth.[12]

Notice, however, that there is a very Greek, western turn to this final stage for Plato. In knowing the "Good" the aspirant knows of its "child," the "Lord of Light." The contemplation of the Good is not simply the understanding of an abstraction but knowledge of a "Lord," a God who himself rules the intelligible world.[13]

For Plato this philosophic path is initially rational and analytic. It is "dialectics" which "gently. . . drags the eye of the soul out of the odious ooze upwards." It is "studies" which help turn "the soul around"(Rep. 533d). For both Plato and Shankara self-mastery and reason are the means of enlightenment.

However, the journey out of the cave, for Plato, is not simply dependent on intelligence. In fact the natural "intelligence of the cave experience is a hindrance of the contemplation of the sun. It is those who are most acute at studying shadows who are the brightest members of the chained cave society" (Rep. 516d). For the philosophic journey Plato has in mind, temperament and will are more crucial than normal intelligence. The journey out of the cave is a highly disciplined event in which patience and endurance are more valuable than ordinary perceptiveness.

It is because of this that Plato expresses a novel idea in the <u>Republic</u>. All those who would be sages in the guardian class must first be soldiers in the warrior class. The athletic and military training in the warrior class is a major preparation for the philosopher-kings of the ideal community.

* * * * *

Eros, loving passion, is the central force for Plato's path of philosophy. It is the very impetus for the ultimate vision of the Good, the ens realissimum of Plato's visionary knowledge. Love is the key, then, for both of the elite classes in the Republic.

There is much confusion about Platonic love. First of all Platonic love is not divorced from physical passion and sexual desire. Plato's description of the lovers in the Phaedrus is some of the most passionate prose in all of Greek literature. (See the whole section, Phaed. 250e-256e.) The lover shudders at the sight of the beloved as at "the sight of a god" (Phaed. 251a). He thinks his lover is a "holy image of deity." His soul "throbs with ferment." There is "aching" and "pain" (Phaed. 251c), a "fever pulse. . . joy . . . anguish." The soul is "perplexed and frenzied. . . with madness."

The lover loves the beloved "above all others . . . mother, brother, friends." The lover tastes "a pleasure that is sweet beyond compare" in the presence of the beloved. The lover forgets "all the rules of conduct, all the graces of life" and welcomes "a slave's estate" (Phaed. 252a). All this Greek lover wants is "any couch" to "lie down close beside her darling." Would anyone confuse this description of love with a brother-sister relationship or a friendship based on intellectual compatibility? It is clear thaat the oragious nature of love is well known by Plato.

In the Symposium, Socrates, quoting Diotima, say that the candidate for "initiation cannot. . . begin too early to devote himself to the beauties of the body" (Symp. 210a). What is the goal of this initiate? It is to be "the friend of God" and "to put on immortality" (Symp. 212a).

"Whoever has been initiated" in "the mysteries of love" is "drawing near the final revelation" (Symp. 210e). Is it clear that Plato is describing sexual attraction to the beauty of body and soul? (He says that "spiritual loveliness" in an "unlovely body" is superior to just physical beauty (Symp. 210c).

This sexual passion, eros, is the force which begins the initiate on a spiritual path to the "eternal oneness" (Symp. 211b). For Plato this mystic path ends with the "final revelation" (Symp. 211c).

Platonic love is deeply rooted in the very wellsprings of physical sexuality. This power of creative eros, however, must be guided and channeled. It must be disciplined by the vision of the philosophic goal. Self-knowledge is part of this process. The beloved "is as it were a mirror" in which "the lover can see himself" (Phaed. 255d). It is also a deeply religious experience. The lover teaches the beloved "to walk in the ways of their God" (Phaed. 253c).

How is sexual power disciplined? It is not disciplined by its denial or removal. In fact the more sexual passion the more impetus for philosophic discovery. For Plato, where there is no passion there is no path. The sexual passion which could be used for ultimate sexual pleasure or procreation must be used by the seeker of philosophic vision for knowledge of the divine. Our "hot blooded" sexual nature must be reined in until the bit splatters the "jaws with blood" (Phaed. 256e).

These "first steps on the celestial highway" (Phaed. 256d) will require an Olympian discipline. It will yield the noblest prize "whether by the vision that is of man or the madness that is of God" (Phaed. 256d). This vision, then, is based on sexual passion without sexual fulfillment. The two lovers, in love, each lead the other on the celibate path of mystic knowledge.

Why would Plato stress chastity and non-orgasmic sex? He speaks in general terms of "incarnations" and of living "righteously," (Phaed. 249a) of eagerness "to be winged" for the journey on the "celestial highway" (Phaed. 256d-e). We may ask why Plato thinks that sex in its most specific form would negate this philosophic journey.

There is a parallel to Plato's thoughts in the right-hand tantric philosophy of India. In India there is a long tradition of sexual continence as a spur to divine enlightenment. The tantric practitioner is encouraged to live as a celibate. Traditional Indian biology and psychology are grounded in certain psychic, emotional, and spiritual "centers." These centers are called "chakras." There are seven chakras in the human body. The lowest chakra is located in the sexual organs. A divine, creative energy comes from this chakra. Its most specific use would be in procreation. In India it is believed that the "sexual" energy used for procreation can be used for the recreation of the individual. The seven chakras are sources of strength, health, love, art, philosophy, courage, and mystical knowledge and power. The celibate can store up the divine energy and, by the practice of yoga, direct the energy into the chakras.

Greek thought seemed to hold similar views. The women who were oracles at the religious centers like Delphi had to be virgins. An athlete preparing for the Olympic games was expected to be celibate during his months of training. Like Plato, Indian tantric philosophy often encouraged the mingling of the sexes in a state of romantic intensity which was meant to be celibate.[14] Romantic intensity would be used as a springboard for enlightenment. The Buddhist cave monasteries at Aurangabad, Ellora, and Ajunta are decorated with sensuous paintings of naked goddesses. The physical beauty of the women was painted alongside the spiritual beauty of the Boddhisattva. The love themes at Ajunta are justly famous for their great delicacy and sensitivity. In cave thirteen the women are displayed in all their coyness, coquetry, and blandishments. The colors are rich, warm, and sensuous, well representing the Gupta renaissance. Throughout the twenty-seven caves there are numerous sculptings of males and females embracing and kissing. (Keep in mind that these caves of exquisite Indian art were monasteries for Buddhist celibates.)[15]

Each Boddhisattva has his female counterpart, his "shakti" or female energy. Had the Buddhist sage, Asanga, assimilated not only the Hindu ideal of Bhakti (personal devotion) but Hindu tantric practice as well? The male and female "blessed ones" are displayed in a relaxed lyrical harmony, a union of celibate sexuality.

(Later on right-hand tantric practices would give way to left-hand tantric practices. Shortly thereafter, around 800 A.D., Buddhism will die out in India.)

Is Plato's chastity-in-love based on something like Indian metaphysics? In the Republic Socrates tells Glaucon that "strong pleasure" must not "beset proper love" (Rep. 403b). The lover is, however, to "touch and kiss" for the sake of "beauty." Then what are we to do with the Socratic remark that "the young men who prove good in warfare...will receive...gifts...prizes..."and "access to the beds of the women" (Rep. 460b)? This access is, however, a special dispensation for the production of children (Rep. 460a). The "best fighter" should, Socrates says, "be in love" (Rep. 468c).

What, then, is the heart of the Platonic doctrine of eros and sexual love? The Platonic scholar Gregory Vlastos says that Plato, by "denying. . . consummation," transmutes "physical excitement into imaginative and intellectual energy." Though "body to body endearment" is always present "terminal gratification will be denied." (See his Platonic Studies, second edition, Princeton University Press, pp. 3-38.)

The purpose for Plato is the same as for the Indian philosophic sage: procreative power used for intellectual transformation instead of procreation. In the Republic this concept is clearly applied to the warrior class (Rep. 403b).

Detachment from illusion is a major tenet of Indian thought. It is especially emphasized in the mystical transcendentalism of Nagarjuna's Buddhist thought, which is so influential in Tibetan philosophy. His emphasis on the relativity of the phenomenal universe and its conditionedness is the key to his moral doctrine of "upaya," or skillful non-clinging (i.e., personal detachment from the unreal). This is the classic Buddhist doctrine of "sunyata" or the relative unreality of the elements of phenomenon. Unlike Plato, Nagarjuna argued against "substances or essences." He taught a doctrine of conditioned becoming comparable to the flux of the pre-Socratic philosopher, Heraclitus. For Nagarjuna all metaphysical systems are simply expressions of the human thirst for the real. Like Shankara, who distinguished the Sagunabrahman who is mixed with "maya" (illusion) from the Nirgunabrahman that is the ground of the universe, Nagarjuna distinguished the "tathata" (the substance of things) from "dharmadhaty" (the ultimate essence) or "bhutakoti" (the apex of reality).

Nagarjuna's anti-metaphysical stance creates a moral climate in which there can be a development of the "bodhisattva" (a saintly sage). If one can see through the illusionary nature of things then one can face all circumstances devoid of doubt, fear, and anxiety, and meet all circumstances with unimpeded insight and unbounded compassion. This is the moral skill of "anutpattika-dharma-ksanta," (the capacity to endure). It is, in the words of K. Venkata Ramanan, "the strength of skillfulness." The bodhisattva is a "mahasattva," one who is invincible, great, and brave. By this detachment from the unreal constructs of the mind's illusions the sage has removed all elements of passion and pride.

There is a comparison between this detachment from the unreality of the world and Plato's distinction between the rational order of ideas and the existential order of the phenomenal world. For Plato the horse that is known by our senses is a copy, or "shadow" of the archetypal horse. Here is an explicit Platonic doctrine which implicitly lays the foundation for a transcendentalist detachment from the shadows of the existential order. The potential guardians would be taught that the "visible forms" of rectangles are the shadows of "the originals they represent" (Rep. 510e). "Knowledge and truth" are not "good, but good like" (Rep. 509a). This Good is "not being but beyond being, surpassing even it in dignity and power" (Rep. 509c).

Since the Good is beyond being, it cannot be an object of metaphysical knowledge. Like Nagarjuna, Plato cannot express this ultimate knowledge with verbal constructs. Like Nagarjuna, Plato's training must prepare the initiate by moral training for this beatific vision. Unlike Nagarjuna, Plato would develop the capacity for this vision by military and athletic discipline. There is no direct Platonic system of meditation or static yoga. There is sport, preparation for war, and artful dialogue with a wise master. Here Greek aggressiveness is distinct from Indian passivity, not in tone, but in style. Plato would be closer to Shankara than to Nagarjuna in his metaphysics. For Nagarjuna metaphysics is only a way of verbal expression. But Shankara, like Plato, provides a positive constructive system as the basis for a personal god ("Ishvara") and individuality in a subject-object epistemology ("visaya-visayi").[16]

However, Nagarjuna, Shankara, and Plato would all agree that the key to their respective dialectical systems is the development of moral character and attitude.[17]

Plato can be justly accused of emphasizing the life of the intellect, with its visionary goal, over the life of the will, with its moral discipline. His famous claim that no one, knowing the Good, would ever do wrong, substantiates this view. Moral knowledge itself would make the auxiliary ethical. This, however, ignores the whole trend of Platonic training in the Republic. Here the training for the golden order of sages is based on years of athletic and military discipline in which the tests of character are emphasized over simple intellectual knowledge. For Plato, the warrior must be the "honor-loving type" (Rep. 583a). His scathing description of the youth raised in democracies (Rep. 559d-564a) is not directed to their intellectual education but to their moral degeneracy. Along with "good memory" Plato wants "doggedness and industry in every sense of the word" (Rep. 535d). "Otherwise," Socrates says, "how do you suppose anyone will consent to undergo the toils of the body and of study and discipline?"

It is because of this that Socrates says that those who would know must be, from their youth up, "athletes of war" (Rep. 521d). For Plato it is "steadfastness," "magnificence in soul," and the "orderly, quiet, and stable" life which must be combined with learning and sagacity if philosophy is to be fruitful (Rep. 503c). It is character which is crucial for success on Plato's philosophic path. The initiate must be "tested in toils, and fears and pleasure" (Rep. 503e). "Sobriety and bravery" must be combined with "justice and wisdom" (Rep. 504a). Labor of mind and exercise of the body are the hard discipline of Plato's military order of the silver knights. (Rep. 504d). For Plato, preparation for the military campaign is preparation for the golden order of sages in his guardian class.

It was this martial character which was the stepping stone for the vision of "the really real reality" (Phaed. 247c). Though they use different methods, it does not seem at this point that Nagarjuna and Plato are far apart in the profundity of their moral emphasis. Here there may be a connection between Tibetan monasticism and the Greek philosophy of Plato's warrior class.

Is Plato's glorification of the military class militaristic? In India, from the advent of the Buddhist tradition, there was a division in sub-continent philosophy concerning the nature of war.

The Hindu scriptures spoke of "ahimsa," non-violence, as the ideal for human behavior. But in the Rig Veda the Brahmins are to be protected. The Ksatriyas (Indian warrior class) must "fight" to protect "the pure." When the Buddha was asked by the warrior Senapati Shinha whether war was ever right the Buddha replied, "He who deserves punishment must be punished." Krishna, after telling Duryodhana what "was truthful, wholesome, and beneficial" discovered that "the fool is not amenable." Only "chastisement by war, danda, the fourth expedient" is proper in this case. In the Bhagavad Gita, Arjuna is taught to fulfill his vocation, "suadharma," and fight. In Indian thought, Radhakrishnan says, "the opposite of love is hate, not force. . . non-violence as a mental state is different from non-resistance." For Indian thought there is a difference between "himsa" or violence and "danda" punishment. Force is the servant of order, "rta." In the Mahabharata the ideal student has his "bow at his back," achieves through "the might of spirit" and the use of "military force" which achieves "its ends." In the <u>Anusasanaparua</u> 231.23, "killing, confining and inflicting pain" can be used to protect "the helpless." In India even Brahmins can be warriors (here we are closer to Plato) as the examples of Parascrama, Dronacarya, and Asuatthama show. In <u>Manu</u> VIII.348 Brahmins are allowed to take up arms, though the highest virtue is still "non-violence." But, Manu says, "one may slay without hesitating a murderous assailant." For the Hindu the key is to fight evil without evil. For Radhakrishnan the non-violent state of war is a state in which "malice and hatred" are absent.

Is Indian thought "militaristic?" Is there a correspondence between Plato's views on the moral justification of a warrior class and Indian thought?

Greek culture was rooted in a warrior code. The Homeric legacy had glorified the warrior cultus. There was nothing major in Greek thought that emphasized the path of non-violence. The sages of the west, Socrates, Plato, and Aristotle, unlike the sages of the east, tended to be married and justify war within certain ethical parameters. The great sages of the east, Shankara, Ramunaja, and Mahdva, were unmarried and held to non-violence, at least as an ideal with certain exceptions.

Plato is the point of compromise between the two cultures. He appropriates philosophic dimensions of both Homeric and Indian traditions. In the <u>Republic</u> Socrates describes aggressive warfare as a solution to possible overpopulation. War, he says, will create a fraternity of warriors, and shared danger will enhance social bonding. No defense is made that such a war is just. He simply describes its utility.

In the <u>Laws</u>, however, he criticizes the barracks life of Sparta (Laws 636b). According to A.E. Taylor, Plato "dissents entirely from" the "ethic of war." In the <u>Laws</u> the Athenian rates "sophrosyne" (balanced, righteous wisdom) above military valor (Laws 631a). It is peace which is the goal of just legislation, first between members of the community, and then between the components of the human soul.

For the mature Plato the warrior is a peacemaker. It is the warrior in both the Indian and Platonic traditions who puts an end to violence and the disruption of justice and peaceful social order. War is the necessary complement of justice and a world of non-violence. The warrior replaces war with peace through war. The technical skill and proficiency of the warrior class is honed to its highest point as a means of re-establishing justice in a world of chaos, confusion, and conflict. It is in the Platonic sense not only a necessary vocation but essentially ethical as well.

* * * * *

Plato's vision of ultimate knowledge is ineffable and mystical. Like Wittgenstein in the <u>Tractatus</u> or the Buddhist negative metaphysics of Nagarjuna in the <u>Maha-Prainaparamita-Shastra</u>, Plato's "agathon" the Good, the ultimate divine knowledge, is unsayable.

Here mystical intuition and vision are reduced to Zen silence. The Platonic scholar Paul Friedländer has said that there can never be a book by Plato or anyone else on "that part of knowledge which is to him most significant." It first of all requires a very special receptiveness of spirit. As in India, the master and disciple would have to live together for a long time to convey this vision of the Ideas (see Plato's Seventh Letter). Knowledge of the ineffable archetype must go by stages, from knowledge of the name, to definition, through image, to transcendental vision. Like Plotinus, Plato would believe that speech about the "beyond being" would "only detract from it by adding." The "dialectical journey" (Rep. 532b) is a journey of knowledge ("logoi"), of love ("eros"), and, finally in the Phaedo, death. As Diotima says, this mystic journey must be taken in "right order and succession" (Symp. 210e). The soul is not to seek this knowledge in introspection but in community. After the hardness of the ascent, the spur of love and desire, something happens "suddenly" (Seventh Letter 341c). In the language of Paul Friedländer, this "cosmic destiny" is a "mystery rite." In the Phaedrus, Plato says that we "were initiated into a mystery that may be truly called most blessed." It is a remembrance of "visions innocent, simple, calm, and blessed, which we beheld in the highest rite, in purest light" (Phaed. 250c). By being "initiated into perfect mystery he becomes truly perfect" (Phaed. 249c). In the language of the Bhagavad-Gita this vision is "like a magician" who penetrates "heart and life (XVIII,55). It corresponds to St. Teresa's illumination which "often comes, like a strong, swift impulse," or Plotinus' soul "suddenly seized by illumination."[18]

Yet this path, Friedländer points out, is not the result of "ecstatic exaggeration," the "compulsion of magic," the dervish dance, or the repetition of mantras and "regulation of breath," or "rigid contemplation." For Plato the path is strictly one of moral and intellectual discipline. It is the result of "affectionate communion with others." It is not the "shapeless Brahma of the Upanishads," but the richness of the Good. It "is to grow in the image of god, beloved of god, and as far as possible, similar to god."

The preparation for this is ten years of military, moral, and athletic training in the class of auxiliaries, or warrior-guardians. It is the development of character or spirit in its most martial sense which prepares the soul for its vision of spirituality, the "arrheton." He who beholds the beautiful finds his meaning in life (Symp. 211d). Training in the silver order of the warrior class prepares the soul for this vision of growing clarity, a vision mediated through mythic imagery.

The ten years spent in the order of silver knights is a preparation for a vision of reality.

What is the vision of reality that is the ultimate goal of Plato's philosophical training? Plato's metaphysics is best expressed in mytho-poetic form. Plato himself does this in the allegories of the cave, the sun, and the chariot. This mytho-poetic language carries with it an impact which is a vehicle of his ontology, his vision of the divine, and the world of sacred ideas. The guardian-warriors are being ultimately prepared for a philosophical mysticism. It is nonetheless a genuine religious mysticism for all of its metaphysical and epistemological implications.

The best way to see this sacred vision is in Platonic myth. In his book The Place of the Lion, the English novelist Charles Williams describes the "hierarchized" celestial orders, powers, virtues, and dominations "which Plato taught his disciples existed in the spiritual worlds." These great principles entered "into aboriginal matter." The protagonist Anthony Durrant is told that the "cold names wisdom, courage, beauty, and strength" are "mighty Powers" angelic in nature. "That which is behind them intends to put a new soul into matter," Mr. Foster says. In Williams' novel, celestial beasts begin to appear in the world. The Powers are the archetypes of these animals.

The wise man, Foster tells Anthony, is the one "who would consecrate himself to this end": to know the nature of these divine Powers. It is "his duty on earth."

In a perfect description of the guardian vocation Williams writes, "all the while to be quiet and steady, to remember that man was meant to control, to be lord of his own nature, to accept the authority that had been given . . . and to exercise that authority over the giants and gods" which threaten the world.

The "Divine Celestials" are hidden in riddles, "lest evil men work sorcery." Under the guise of the sacred eagle, the lion, the unicorn, the crowned snake, the butterfly, the phoenix, the horse, and the lamb, these divine ideals manifest themselves to the bewildered gaze of Williams' characters. These angelic universals were given, Williams writes, for "the authority of men." The "strong and lovely knowledge which was philosophy" taught that "Powers were walking about on the earth."

The forms of "the strength of the lion and the subtlety of the crowned serpent, and the loveliness of the butterfly, and the swiftness of the horse" were manifested in the existential order of space, time, and matter. These beasts were "hints and expressions of lasting things," of "the Divine Ones" who "exist in their own blessedness." They came from "the place of the foundations." (It is the "power of death" to him who has "never governed" these powers "in himself.")

In the understanding of Williams' Platonic mystic, Richardson, a new vision of reality emerges in the vision of horses. He saw "for the first time in this new world of appearance the union of high power for high ends." He also realizes the ultimate Platonic gnosis: ". . . one form, and only one." His mind is led in the way of negation "in a perpetual aspiration beyond even the Celestials to that which created the Celestials."

This knowledge is a transforming experience for Williams' characters. It brings to them "that beauty of innocence which is seen in unhappy mankind only in sleep and death and love and transmuting sanctity—the place of the lamb in the place of the lion."

Williams' initiates discover that "beauty went with strength and subtlety, and made haste to emotion as to mind, to sense as to spirit . . . and speed."

The "movement of the eagle was the measure of truth." There were other royal creatures of "perpetually renovated beauty, a rosy glow, a living body," and "the wonder of earthly love." These Ideas were "the inmost life of the universe . . . instinct with strength," subtlety, beauty, and speed. In Williams' novel this vision comes in the form of a "blazing Phoenix" sweeping from its "nest of fire." The "interfused Virtues" that came with the Phoenix "made a pattern of worlds" and "brought forth living creatures to cry out one moment for joy and then be swallowed in the Return." It was an "ephemera of eternity" that "broke into being."

For Williams' characters on their quest for understanding, this knowledge could ultimately be found "only to the spirit in solitude." But some of these things could be discovered "only to a man in companionship." Only philosophic companionship could give the most important grace, "balance." No one's mind was so good that it did not need another mind to counter and equal it . . . to "save it from conceit and blindness and bigotry and folly."

Only this communal balance could give the philosopher on the path "humility which was a lucid speed." It was "movement in balance" that was "the truth of life, and the beauty in life." For Williams, the initiate on the quest for the knowledge of philosophic foundations must "offer up his being to divine Philosophy." He must see "the balance in things—Lion and Lamb, the Serpent and the Phoenix, the Horse and the Unicorn: ideas as they were visualized and imagined." For these voyagers "friendship was one, but friends were many; the idea was one, but its epiphanies many."

The mystic knowledge learned by Williams' characters was knowledge known by "the spiritual intellect" which "beheld by their fashioned material bodies the mercy which hid in matter" because "man was not yet capable of naked vision." All of this poetry was the approach of the "fallen understanding to that unfallen meaning." And yet the path for these people had its terror and dangers. In Williams' words, "whoever denied that austere godhead, wherever and however it appeared—its presence, its austerity, its divinity—refused" to be human. It was a rejection of his "high spiritual mastery" and the "discovery of himself."

In Williams' powerful fictive language we have a mythic picture of Plato's vision of the true, the Good and the beautiful. The philosophic ideas of Plato's metaphysics were not meant to be bloodless abstractions but transformational inspirations for the philosophic soul. Both his warriors and guardians, in the class of auxiliaries, were preparing body, mind, and character as receptacles for knowledge of these mysteries. Here the life of the intellect and the life of the spirit coincided with all of its potential glory and its grave dangers.

* * * * *

For Plato, military training and war are not ends in themselves. He ultimately rejects the values of the Spartan state. In the Laws, (631c) Plato, speaking through the Athenian, ranks two types of goods. In the natural order it is health, beauty, athletic strength, and the just use of wealth. In the "divine" order it is wisdom ("Sophrosyne"), discipline of spirit, righteousness, and (fourth!) valor.

For Plato, true martial valor is not simply the ability to face danger and pain; it also means the ability to overcome the seductions of pleasure, "which melt the mettle of the would-be precisian like so much wax" (Laws 633d). For Plato, true martial development must train the warrior's character to not only face the dangers of war but the dangers of the moral life and its seductions.

The corporate training of the future guardians and warriors in Plato's silver military order would be a moral and philosophical path, a Tao or way of self discovery as well as a vita contemplativa. It was a sacred pilgrimage whose goal was the refinement of the self in conjunction with the transcendent.

The philosopher was first a military hero. His character was extensively tested. In the Republic Socrates says that the "young guardians must be exposed. . .to both terrors and pleasures." He would "test them more rigorously than gold in fire." The Platonic philosophic master would see if these young warriors could "resist beguilement" and "keep their composure at all times." He would find out if they were "proper guardians" of themselves before they became either military professionals or guardians of the republic (Rep. 413e). In the Gorgias Socrates describes an athletic discipline which would develop gracefulness, agility, and active manliness. In the Timaeus Plato describes an "exercise" of the soul. This exercise will discipline the individual to be in touch with "the divinity within him" (Tim. 90c). This initiate must "exercise his intellect more than any other part of him." Thus he will cherish divine power and "be immortal." He will be raised up from earth to the "kindred who are in heaven" (Tim. 90a). To achieve this, the body and soul must be brought into a harmonious balance. If the body is weak and the soul is strong, or if the body is strong and soul is weak, there will be discord (Tim. 87e-90d). Beauty is absent because there is no "due preparation of mind and body." Of all the ways of purifying the body, "the best is gymnastics" (Tim. 88e).

This journey, then, is a physical, mental, and spiritual quest. Joseph Campbell, in his book The Hero With a Thousand Faces, describes the spiritual principles and universal doctrines in the development of the heroic self. It corresponds to Plato's philosophic journey in the warrior class. The first test is the call to adventure. The budding hero and heroine must leave the place of safety and risk themselves in an unknown world. They must go to an alien land, leave home, be born, and enter the threshold experience. They must face the mysterious guardian powers of the cosmos. There are numerous tests of character. In Greek, "peira" means a test by which the voyager establishes quality of character. Wrong roads, demonic power, moral failure, numerous imagined and real dangers are all part of a spiritual boot camp. They must often rely on helpers, priests, hermits, spirits, and forest hags.

There are many tests in preparation for the supreme ordeal, a moment of self-sacrifice and rebirth. In the Odyssey, Odysseus must leave the beauty, comfort, and pleasure of Circe's bed, overcome the lure of the sirens, and resist the temptations of the lotus-eaters.

For Homer, success comes from courage, strength, ingenuity, restraint, patience, tact, self-control, and, above all, the will to go home. It is the Greek ideal at its highest. It incorporates Penelope, Akhilles, and Arthur. It is a Platonic archetype of character for Plato's elite classes: warrior and sage.

For a Greek like Homer, the real enemies of the spiritual quest are unreasoned curiosity and the uncontrolled appetites of our passions.

For Joseph Campbell, the hero is the one who, while still alive, knows the claims of the super conscious, which is more or less unconscious in the ordinary person.[19] This hero of self-forgetful valor and balanced soul is a perfect description of Plato's auxiliaries.

Platonic discipline, in Campbell's language, would be the text of the rites of passage. The knowledge of this mythic journey is an ultimate truth of which the human limited experience is a temporal reflection. It is to reveal through mortal things the brilliance of the eternal form. The religious imagery of Plato is the human conceptual framework of the play of eternity in time.

The balancing of the body through the ritual of exercise and the balance of temperament in the self is a Platonic military ideal. It is typified in Walter Otto's description of the Homeric legacy: the mastery of the moment and the divine precision of the well planned deed.

Socratic knowledge is aesthetic in its very core. It is this very experience of beauty which is the center of Plato's rational mysticism. It would cause, in Friedrich von Schiller's language, a true "disinterestedness." Beauty for Schiller was a form of "play." It was central to human self-knowledge and to human repose and total freedom. It was the ground of the innate human principles of harmony. It is easy to see in all of this nineteenth century romanticism the influence of Plato. The Socratic emphasis on eros and the movement of the soul toward beauty is the fabric of aesthetical romanticism in Johann Fichte, Schiller, and Friedrich Schelling. What is the intimation of beauty like for Plato?

The archetypical nature of the vision of the agathon may be best expressed by C.S. Lewis in his children's novel <u>The Magician's Nephew</u>. Digory and Polly meet a mysterious lion, a symbol of divine transcendence in a world of magic. The children, looking up into the lion's face, undergo a transforming experience. The face of the lion seems to change to "a sea of tossing gold," and "such sweetness and power rolled about them and over them and entered into them that they felt they had never really been happy or wise or good, or even alive and awake before." The impact was unforgettable. The recollection "of that moment stayed with them always, so that as long as they both lived… the thought of all that golden goodness… was still there, quite close, just around some corner." This memory "would come back and make them sure, deep down inside, that all was well," when they were sad, or afraid, or angry.

In an artistic sense this is a description of the Socratic vision. The aesthetic experience of beauty conveys the knowledge of agathon. It is Friedrich Schelling's "idea of beauty." Schelling believed that it was the aesthetic character of our consciousness of beauty which was the highest act of reason. The intellectual intuition which combines art, mythology, religion, and philosophy was, for Schelling, the bridge to the absolute. Here there is a turning out "towards the other." Simple self-reflection is in Schelling's words, "a spiritual malady." We are born for action, he says, and action is the primal result of aesthetic reflection. It is "art," the seminal beauty of nature, the intuition of aesthetical experience, which gives us the key to our poetic existence. The aesthetically guided imagination gives us the knowledge of divine expressions and sacred intimations. Like Plato, Schelling grounded human knowledge and hope on the notion of divine ideas whose beauty rested in their participation in those ideas. It is these ideas that the philosopher must intuit directly. Beauty is the finite manifestation of the infinite absolute. Like Schelling, Plato would never divorce rationality from the roots of rationality in the world of sacred ideas. (This may be why Plato believed that the members of the warrior class should be in love.)

Action, involvement in the precarious twists and turns of history in war or culture, is the moral outgrowth of this Socratic vision. For Polly and Digory it is the moral quality of the vision of the lion which anchors their spirit in the pressures of combat.

* * * * *

The conscious vision of Plato's divine ideals is not necessarily imaginatively contentless. Because of the distinction in Plato's thought between material things in space and ideal things of pure being, it might be assumed that ideal things are purely conceptual with no "visionary" elements whatsoever. But the influence of Parmenides on Greek idealism allows for a less dramatic separation in Platonic thought between the sensuousness of conscious experience and matter. The vision of the Good, the experience of ultimate consciousness, does not have to be a visionary blank simply because the terms of present sense experience have no referential value for the wordless ultimate. Must we believe that the transformational splendor of the Platonic ideal is simply analytic in nature, like the conceptual relationships of a syllogism? It seems more accurate to say that the conscious imagery of the totally other is if anything more dramatic in its richness than the ordinary consciousness of our existing world. This is the whole point of the allegorical language of the cave and the painfully beautiful enlightenment of the sunlight. Here the distinction between conception and perception may not hold, but blend into, a higher poetic understanding that can only be expressed tangentially toward the heart of the knower. It would be a wordless pointing through myth to the ineffably sacred mystery. The experience of this referent of pointing is the cause of ideal embodiment in consciousness. In dialectical reciprocity only the megalopsuchos (the "great souled individual," according to Aristotle) can receive this knowledge, while at the same time it is this knowledge which makes the visionary great souled. This connecting point of vision and character is a slumbering polarity of richness, receptivity, and reflection.

It is the striving for this knowledge which would create in Plato's warriors the virtue of sophrosyne. The balanced restraint of passion and appetite, the modesty and genuine pride free from vanity, the respectful deportment in the presence of significance, valor and firmness, the wholesomeness of one's spirit, are all grounded in the warrior's soul through a renaissance of divine intimations. In the words of Aristotle, this life would make us immortal if we would "exert ourselves to live in accordance with what is best in us" (Ethics, 1178a). It would create a climate for valor. For Aristotle the most noble courage is found in the most noble death, a death in battle. "There you have the greatest and the noblest danger." It is a valor which occurs "most particularly in warfare" (Ethics, 1115b).

Would this military valor best come from moral training based on Plato's sacred knowledge? The whole trend of Plato's thoughts affirms that direction.

Time and place in war are the shadows of justice in the eternal dimension. Battle is the cosmic gateway for the birth of peace, order, and justice. The scarring and maiming of war is the temporal display of the valorous attributes in the interior life of the spirit. It is the warrior who stands in the threshold of fear and pain and activates the transcendent Good incarnationally at the moment of moral significance. The historic moment of terror, pain, and death is the redressing temporal balance of fate in the crisis of historic moral exploitation. The warrior is both the catalyst and instrument of this sacred return of harmony, poise, and the eternity of justice in the mundane affairs of enriched commonplaces in their natural rhythms. War is the sacrificial offering of all that is most dear in the redemptive process of historic fallenness. The act of battle is the enshrinement of the Platonic ideal in the warrior's heart, itself filled with vision and spirit. Death in battle would be the crystallization of transcendence in an existence which mirrors the valorous aspect of being.

* * * * *

What would the members of Plato's warrior class be like? What, in essence, is the mystic visionary who is also a warrior? The crusader Tancred is a model of the Platonian knight. Digby records that his parents' riches did not move him to luxury nor did the power of his family move him to pride; that when young he had the maturity of the old, preferring prayer to sleep and labor to rest. To be with Tancred, thought his soldiers, was to be in safety, and the army would not be like an army if he was not there.

In the western ideal, Tancred corresponds to the neo-Confucian ideal of "sageliness within, kingliness without," to use Jon Wetlesen's phrase. The sageliness or wisdom of the fighting professional in this case is a type of moral wisdom. Tancred first must know how to be so that he can know how and what to do.

This knowledge of what to do is released by his being in harmony with the ontological realities of objective ethical properties. The military professional is the final and ultimate source of the existential establishment of value. Spinoza proposes, as Zen practioneer Paul Wienphal suggests, that Divinity is activity. Here is the philosophical possibility of connecting the spiritual nature of the military professional as the divine vocation of protecting the existing and the activity of Spinoza's "creative power."

Both activities are divine tasks—God's in the absolute sense of Spinoza's power for existence, the warrior's in the secondary but still divine sense of protection of the divinely existent. To refuse to defend the divinely manifested existing is to deny the moral imperative of sharing in creating. It is to be indifferent to the possibility of "being" slipping into "nonbeing." The ideal portrait of Tancred is a representation of the essential character necessary for the task of preservation. To protect the divine establishment of existence as the God-willed manifestation of being as such, the warrior must himself be God-like or quasi-divine. Tancred's divine character is the projection of Divine Activity in existence and involvement through submissive willingness. Describing the theological science of the twelfth century Christian masters, M.-D. Chenu suggests that St. Paul speaks of Christ as the "character" of the divine hypostasis whose eternal character can be imprinted on our rational soul. In miniature, the knight Tancred, (to borrow a phrase from St. Athanasius) is a Homo Dominicus, a "Man-Lord," of the universe. It is this character of the Man-Lord that is the essence of his knighthood.[20]

In praise of the crusader, Godfrey of Bouillon, it was said that he was bountiful to the poor, merciful to the faulty, humble, human, self-disciplined, just and chaste. One would have thought him, it is remarked, the light of monks instead of the general of armies, for he was prayerful and firm in his word. Refusing to be King of Jerusalem after the first crusade he was the model for all kings in his self-abnegation.

To be a knight like Godfrey is to be human in the fullest sense of metaphysical manifestation in ideal archetypical essence. It is to have the imago Dei as the ground of selfhood, as the ever-changing Act in temporal stability.

Shankara describes the God-filled man as a lion: kingly, lordly, and noble. The German mystic Eckhart describes him as God-like and masterful. In That Hideous Strength, C.S. Lewis describes his spiritual heroes and heroines as lion-like as they walk about their ordinary duties, free and fearless even as "they sprawled in their chairs—as if they were the lords of the universe."

J.R.R. Tolkien's Hobbits are perfect literary examples of the development of military power and strength. Meek and fearful, they enter upon high adventure facing the power and might of a world falling to evil. Undersized and innocent, they seem no match for the malevolence and cunning of the wicked. All along the way they suffer from cold, hunger, and thirst, from sudden attacks, from missed paths and silly mistakes, from fear and homesickness, desertion, and illness, the evil in their own natures, and failures induced by temptation. In short, they are knightly models on Plato's royal road. But there comes a day when they come home victorious. Now they are tall and fearless, majestic in their well-earned power. They are man-lords of the universe. They can never again be content with mediocrity. They have spent their lives in giving power away, in giving away what all evil desires most and, in doing so, have become rich in soul and spirit.

The Hobbits suddenly realize that the common crowd look on them with fear and amazement. They had become so used to warfare that they had forgotten their bright mail, the magnificent helmets of Gondor and the Mark, and the shields engraved with knightly emblems. They are a cut above the common man for they are warriors of high spirit and yet so self-forgetful that they are surprised and moved at the awe of the weak.

They return home from the terrible yet enriching journey to the ends of the earth, only to find their home in the shire controlled by the regulators, the dictators, the exploiters of weakness and innocence. They find a society with petty rules, orc-talk, fear and lack of self-determination.

They are under arrest, they are told by the police, for gate breaking, tearing up the rules, trespassing, bribing guards with food, and ignoring the orders of the big man, Sharkey.

"And what else?" Frodo asks mockingly.

"That'll do. . ." the sheriff says.

"I can add some more if you like," says the intrepid soldier Sam. "Calling your chief names, wishing to punch his pimply face, and thinking your sheriffs look a lot of tom-fools."

These Hobbits can laugh at the petty dictators of the world, for they have brought down the kingdoms of evil with their own purity, courage and innocence.

"You're to come along quiet," they are told. "We're going to take you. . .and hand you over to the chief's men."

The Hobbits roar with laughter.

"Don't be absurd," Frodo says, "I am going where I please, and in my own time." And the masterful Hobbits publicly tear up the rules and regulations.

In the face of evil there is no self-doubt, but rather self-assertion. The great warriors' cloaks are cast back, out flash the deadly swords, and the sunlight shines on the silver and sable of the royalty of Gondor. The ruffians give back. Scaring Breeland peasants and bullying bewildered Hobbits had been easy. But it was another matter to face these fearless Hobbits with bright words, grim faces, and intrepid spirits.

The meek, humble, and innocent of the earth became great lords and bold lions flashing forth power. They had dedicated all of their quavering strength in the service of light and goodness, and they became the mighty, royal princes of a cleansed world.

The pitiful little strength had multiplied into radiating power. The meek and humble Hobbits had not only conquered the earthly kingdoms of evil but had done the much harder task of developing their spirit. Middle Earth was turned upside down, and the meek had inherited the earth. In the Hobbits, the Warrior and the Saint had developed in the same temporal process.

* * * * *

It is very easy to underestimate the importance of the existential order of human events in Plato's thought. Not much has been said about the value of the "shadow world" for Plato. In the allegory of the cave the philosopher re-enters the cave. The shadows of reality, of course, are far inferior to their prototypes. Yet the value of involvement in the shadow world has more value than the perpetual vision of the archetypes. The whole purpose of a warrior class is the defense of the existing city of justice which is itself a shadow of the divine ideals. Though the soul is superior to the body, the body has a high value in Plato's thought. For erotic love and athletic training, the physical world is the ground of spiritual ascent. Because the archetype has more value in a hierarchy of being, we do not have to assume that the shadow, the copy, lacks critical importance even though it is below the archetype. The members of the warrior classes will spend their lives amidst the shadows of war and carnage in defense of a justice hidden in the shadow world. Nothing could show more the value with which Plato gilds the events of time and human action. These warriors, though professionals in one sense, are really morally trained humanists in another sense. Art, poetry, sport and philosophy "drill" their soul while they learn the war drill of combat maneuvers. It was Aristotle who had argued that citizen soldiers fight more bravely than competent professionals without heart (*Ethics*, 116b). At the battle of Coronea in the Sacred War, the citizens fought to the death against the Phocians (353 B.C.) because they feared disgrace more than defeat.[21] This training of the soul with transcendental values is put at the service of the world as it is.

* * * * *

I would like to suggest that Plato's idea of using military and athletic training in his warrior class was not primarily for the development of a Greek soldier. The elite military auxiliaries are certainly meant to be paid professionals in every sense, disciplined in character, and proficient in the use of weapons. However, I think that Plato had a goal in mind other than the martial preparation of his male and female silver knights. The Platonic ideal was the integration of the self with the divine agathon (the Good). It was "knowledge of the well-constituted in the well-constituted" (Seventh Letter, 343e). The preparation for war was a means to a specific philosophic end, the philosopher mystic who would enrich the polis with a transcendent wisdom. More than this, however, was the emanation of this wise vision and noble character throughout the Greek community.

For Plato, the life of the philosopher was a warfare. In Plato's thought, the fragile existence of the Greek warrior in the clash of shield and spear was exceeded by the prospective guardian's internal warfare for liberation from chains, darkness, and the cave.

The true philosopher, like the mature Socrates among the Athenians, was as much at hazard as the young spear-wielding Socrates was in the war against Sparta. In the Symposium we see Socrates, the ultimate philosopher king, in the midst of drink and sexual temptations. In the Phaedo we see the self-possessed Socrates facing death while all grieve around him. The old Socrates who will not flee the death sentence and the injustice of his fate is more noble than the young hero who faced the fearsome spear tips in battle before the walls of Potidaea in 431.

I am suggesting that the Platonic training in the Republic was meant to be a training for life. It was meant to be for all people to some degree and for the men and women in the guardian class in a pre-eminent degree. Warfare in the phalanx was a preparation for moral war, the care of one's soul, and the development of the Greek ideal in human existence. For Plato, Socrates is an ideal, and training in the auxiliaries a preparation for that ideal. Military might was a by-product of the moral alchemy and philosophical wizardry of the Platonic charisma and its spiritual vision.

Arnold Toynbee has said that all histories resemble the Iliad. If you read it as history it will be full of fiction but if you read it as fiction you will find it full of history.[22] (It was Aristotle who argued that good fiction is the truth about human relationships.) Plato's thoughts were infused with a pre-philosophic atmosphere of Homeric thought. It is to Homer that he so often turns for a phrase or a quick quote. His notion of the warrior ethos comes, in part, from the mythic world views of this ultimate Greek poet. In Homer's Iliad, The Shield of Victory, Kenneth John Atchity explores this Greek warrior ethos in depth. I believe he and Walter Otto have mined the rich veins of the Homeric spirit, extracting the martial ethos of early Greek thought that embroidered Plato's implicit notions of a warrior class. The Homeric models of Akhilles and Hektor, community and companionship, and the action of the gods, are all precursors of Plato's military ideas.

Akhilles is the epitome of the Greek warrior. The fabric of cosmic order has been torn by the violation of hospitality and the rupturing of the marriage tie. The Trojan prince, Paris, has been the instigator of the break in ties of friendship and guest relationship. In this act of treachery, Paris is defended by the Trojan people. This defense of disorder will seal the fate of Troy.

According to Kenneth Atchity, the warrior, in the Homeric sense, has a social consciousness which is developed out of an "awareness of historic continuity."

The Homeric warrior must be willing to defend the national collective, itself based on value and moral order. One generation of men will grow "while all men must eventually die," Glaukus says (Iliad, 6.144-51).

To Homer, even the gods are warriors. Apollo is a god walking with a silver bow and hooded quiver, the shafts clashing angrily on his shoulders with every step. He attacks "like descending night" (Iliad 1.43-52). Along with the rest of the gods, he is concerned with the human affairs and their wars. Apollo will punish the Achaians for Agamemnon's communal transgressions and the slighting of the priest class, as represented in Greek religious faith and practice. It is as if the gods are agents in human affairs (Iliad 4.84). Through systems of rewards and punishments they guide society toward the golden order of the gods. Homer sees the tight connection between the divine and the mundane, between the collective nature of human community and its heroic individual manifestations like Akhilles, the Greek hero and defender of moral relationships violated by the community of Troy.

If Artemis is the archetypical heroine of purity and chastity, Helen's fatal beauty is the source of disorder, suffering and death. She is the crystallized confusion of social order. According to Atchity, she will be the center of disordered societal meaning, a vortex around which Paris, Priam, Andromache and Hektor will spin to their destruction.

Each will search through a course of action for some solution. The gods, however, have irreversibly doomed Troy. Paris is the symbol of the perpetual eroticist. As the lord of the "lovely-haired Helen," Paris is ambitious without power, weak, passive and rebellious. The young boxer of Troy was not always so enervated. It was only after his fatal love for Helen that his mind turned from the hard tasks of combat to the pleasures of the bed. Hektor will refer to him as woman-crazy, cajoling, better to have never been born(Iliad 3.39-40). For Homer, even the handsomeness of Paris is itself sinister, since it has no relevance to order and justice but serves its opposite. He has violated the orderly nature of social bonds. Thus, in the Homeric view, the continued health of all societies demands the annihilation of Troy. Paris, unlike Menelaus, lacks even the virtue of courage. Menelaus, claiming divine sanction from Zeus himself, curses all Trojans for the loss of his wife to Paris. In this early Greek world of war and chaos, manhood is defined by the warrior ethos. King Priam of Troy sees too late that his refusal to punish the deed of his weak son leads directly to the death of the beloved and glorious Hektor. The valorous and well-ordered life of Prince Hektor is not sufficient to reverse the disorderliness of the Trojan cause.

In Homer's portrayal of the Trojan hero Hektor, we see, on one level, a fighting professional of supreme virtue. He is the chief prince, whose charisma and leadership hold family and community together. In Troy, this warrior and the values he defends are a matter of age and gender. His "virility and domesticity are complementary." Hektor realizes that glory is a national value. He feels the heavy load of the essential goodness of social responsibility. Zeus, the lord of the cosmos in the Iliadic world, has ordained Hektor to be a protector of Troy. In one moment of recklessness, he takes the offensive and kills Patroklos, violating his divine commission by being the aggressor. Now Akhilles, the one human with divine power to defeat him will re-enter the war. Hektor, because he is fighting against the Achaians, who are fighting for cosmic order, must lose. In a moment of tragic moral lapse he ". ..believed in his own strength and ruined his people" (Iliad 22.104-10).

Hektor, the breaker of horses, will become an example of loyalty and duty to family and culture. The gods honor and bless his nobility, but not his cause. They honor the transcendental nature of goodness and character but he cannot be a victorious hero.

Akhilles is the catalyst of military action and the restoration of order. He is the instrument of the vengeance of the gods. He is the restorer of the cosmic ties in the unique acts of military heroism.

As Atchity points out, Homeric thought sees Akhilles as a powerful "self" which crystallizes and motivates action. He makes the future by moral act. The world will not be the same because of him. It is a harmonious, though unconscious, cooperation of the gods and the world. It is, in this ancient Greek view, the sword arm of Akhilles which is the central means of making history.

As a warrior, Akhilles must define his relationship to political authority. Agamemnon has unlawfully taken his booty, his prize of war, the young Briseis. Will Akhilles fight for a king who thus breaks the laws of gods and men? He decides at first not to do so. Only when his cousin and companion Patroklos is killed by Hektor does he see his mistake. The issue of the injustice done to him must be subordinate to the greater cause of cosmic order. In the murky moral issues of justice and war, maturity demands action even where both sides are not free of fault.

It is brotherhood which begins to call him to his senses. Atchity, quoting Rachel Bespaloff's <u>On the Iliad</u>, points out that it is not through action that human nature is revealed at its most profound level. It is instead the choosing of our loves. What we love is how we act. Akhilles must love justice more than Briseis. He will fight for the more righteous against the less righteous, out of an initial moment of moral insight caused by his love and loyalty to friendship. His just anger against the king had turned to a misguided use of his divine gifts. He is a warrior, not a king. As Kenneth Atchity points out, Akhilles' role as a warrior is as important to the social collective as the artist. They are protectors of value. In fact ". . .the medicinal function of the warrior logically precedes that of the poet; physical well-being provides the basis. . ." for the arts. Because of brotherhood, his valor becomes a universal motif of action.

The death of Patroklos in this war is the spur to just revenge on Hektor and Troy. Zeus, in his foresight, has given Akhilles a charisma that will crystallize justice in the act of revenge, necessary for the maintenance of universal goodness and right. This primal urge for revenge served a social, historic, cosmic, and moral good.

Akhilles becomes that primitive force for the restoration of order. One society must obliterate another through the necessarily flawed heroism of Akhilles. In the Homeric concept, the just rage of Zeus is infused as fighting power in the agent of justice. Aeneas tells Apollo that no one can fight Akhilles because Akhilles is supported by the force of order itself (Iliad 20.97-99).

The renewed orderliness of Akhilles is seen first in the healing of community with the athletic events. These sports are a divine means of creating social cohesion through friendly, but intense, competition. Private instruction, society, and brotherhood have created Akhilles. He has been developed by the gods through community. He must now be the agent of social healing. He praises Agamemnon for his valor. Akhilles, in Atchity's view, must accept the king for the virtues he has rather than reject him for his defects. Sport and game are the means of this moral healing. In Homer's view, games enhance the ability to fight by stressing communal cooperation. They are an outlet for human tensions, and like drama, serve as a katharsis. To use Atchity's phrase, "justice, in the established rules of athletic competition, heals all wounds. . ." because it must be "tempered with mercy. . ."

Thus, when the battle fury is over, and Akhilles has served his sacred role, he will return the body of Hektor to Priam for decent burial. Akhilles, flawed to some extent by the passions of war, skates on the brink of "losing his humanity." The gods must act to prevent this dangerous tragedy. Apollo (now with the lyre, the symbol of harmony, not the bow, the symbol of war) argues that Akhilles is a lion, blinded by a wrath that no longer serves order. Akhilles cannot be allowed to ignore the laws of Zeus that are fundamental to human order.

Cedric Whitman (quoted by Atchity) points out that Akhilles' heroism is really a search for the "dignity and meaning of the self." He wishes, in Charles Beye's thought, to break through natural limitations and realize his true nature. This pursuit of glory, in the historic order, which could become self-centered and self-destructive, becomes a transcending value when allied, first to friendship, and secondly to the restoration of order. In Atchity's phrase it is a "communal virtue," a tool by which society insures competition (in sports) and military action. Akhilles must "abnegate his selfhood and individual prowess" for the good of communal value before he can find himself.

The dignity and meaning of the moral self of Akhilles is found at its most healing and highest moment in the honor he shows the dead Hektor and his father, King Priam. Akhilles transcends the quarrels of historic systems and political communities. The act of mercy, after the war has settled the issues at hand, is an affirmation of the dignity of transcendental human nature. It is this supreme affirmation of human dignity which transcends the partisanship of war. It is pity, Atchity argues, which is the ultimate commitment of life. Quoting Thomas Green's interpretation of Homer's world view, Atchity points out that, "The Achaian warrior's antagonist is not so much the Trojan as it is death itself, and time, flux, oblivion, mutability, operating within the gray ironic perplexities of that dim world." Glory, in this sense, is the perpetuation of societal continuity and the value of cosmic order for these Greeks. It is not war and force as such that is glory, but the restoration of order, value, social ties, and the dignity of innate, God-like, humanity. The victor must heal, and in healing bring the defeated back into the system of communal value. Apollo must set aside the bow and take up the harp. In Charles Beye's words, the very antithesis of the civilized arts: hate, confusion, and death, must be replaced by "music, dancing and oratory." Defiling the body of Hektor, Akhilles is on the verge of destroying social value. His redemption comes with the return of his Apollonian humanity and the honoring of fatherhood in the person of Priam. It is in the existential sense, the knowledge of his own father's grief for Akhilles' future death, which touches him with the maturing pain of moral knowledge and insight.

Retribution and love of glory are affirmed by Homer as divine tools in historic processes. These motives, when guided by lawful obedience to the divine and legitimate social authority, have value. They are types of gods.

In the picture of Akhilles himself we see a paradigm of the warrior's problems: how can he be the central cosmic agent of the communal destruction of evil and, at the same time, preserve his intrinsic humanity? He is self-centered, cruel, and rebellious. He must become altruistic, humane and obedient. Love in friendship, obedience to sacred vocation in the use of his divine gifts, and the strong awareness of his own mortality and failings are the key to glory and the divine discovery of his real nature.[23]

* * * * *

These insights of Homer may give us a hint as well as a key to human history and its relationship with war. Here the work done by the Greek classicist Walter Otto can be insightful. According to Otto, the Homeric view is first of all a deeply poetic and, therefore, religious view of the universe. For Homer the events of military history depend on a high sensitivity to the "heavenly presence."

In the Greek view of Homer, military events are connected with the action of "the gods" (theoi) or "God" (theos). Menelaus says that all victorious actions are in the hands of the immortal gods. Hektor, though not Akhilles' equal, is willing to say that despite the superiority of his enemy, victory "lies upon the knees of the gods." How, specifically, does Homer think the divine powers work in the time, space, and matter of actual history?

According to Walter Otto, Homer's genius essentially resides in a direct insight into the nature of "divine happening." Deity is in the world and "meets man out of the things of the world." It is not by turning inward that God is met. It is by proceeding outward, by action. It is heroic action that brings us the "immediacy of divine encounter."

Walter Otto believes that here the Greek and Indian views may part, at least by emphasis if not by degree. The Greek emphasis is on the Homeric "outward." The Homeric view emphasizes the "objective and substantial." The "subjective" modes of human consciousness, the attitudes and thoughts of honor, prudence, moderation, tenderness, charm and justice are first and foremost divine realities. In Aristotle's phrase they must be known by "allo genos gnoseos," another kind of understanding than the rational. Resolution in action is based on insight, on the knowledge of divine vision in the individual consciousness. Knowledge, attitude, the significant action, is first objectively divine and then subjectively human.

It is Zeus's daughter Athena, born out of his head, who gives to the heroes "clarity of vision" and "mastery of the moment," acuteness, and shrewdness. Odysseus' wisdom and cleverness is an inspiration from his heavenly escort. Athena's hidden voice is the root of his free and conscious action. At a moment of doubt, the goddess saves the wavering Diomedes with the "decisive thought and saving resolution." She gives Akhilles self-mastery in a moment of vision as he is about to attack Agamemnon. He goes for his sword, is touched from behind, and sees the "divinely lighted eyes of the goddess as she motions him to desist." The aged Phoenix says that it was some god who stopped his rashness at a decisive moment. Some thought invaded his soul with power, a thought produced by deity. The very "subjective" ground of psychic life is rooted in the objective actions of deity. The shipwrecked Odysseus gives Athena the credit for helping him keep his wits about him.

In the Iliad, Homeric heroes are always under the influence of the divine. A brave man, deserted by his god, must run. Patroklos is infused with a high spirit which leads him to die. Yet his death brings Akhilles back into the struggle for justice. All this, then, these acts of history, are in the hands of the gods.

These insights of Homer, according to Walter Otto, reveal the consciousness of divinity on the part of a nation of heroes "unparalleled in all the world." It is, for the Greek, a lively awareness of the divine in rational clarity and the passion of heroism. No cast of the spear, no thrust of the sword can succeed without the cooperation of divinity. In Sophocles' Ajax, the powerful hero forgets his father's words and tries to win without respect for the gods. He fails tragically. It is the gods who bring good fortune, strength and power. They bring a "wonderful quickness, a capacity to act, manfulness and intelligence." Homer's concept of act, according to Otto, is not some fixed inward thing, but a gift and expression of a divine manifestation. Every act is based on the world forces manifested in the "significant event," the eternal forms of which come from the gods.

The gods cause one person to be wise in council, another to love ships, javelins and arrows. The god Zeus gives Hektor force and strength in his inward body, not as an intrinsic power, but for the glorious moment. Why do the gods choose now one, now another? Otto, quoting Schiller, emphasizes that merit and fortune are interrelated. God is not "inside" man but outside, "upon the way." Man must start if he is to encounter the divine through heroic action. It is not by miracle or luck that victory is ultimately won. Upon the elect and enlightened, the divine comes at the historic moment's supreme significance in battle.

In Homer's view it is not merely in the "subjective" modes of consciousness that the divine plays on the fields of history. In war itself the gods are present though normally unseen. The internal empowering of fortitude and strength is combined with divine presence. It is the gods that are the "facilitating factors of human undertakings." It is not only the triumph over infirmity and weariness of the internal life, or the restoration of vitality and heroic spirit, but the presence of the gods on the very battlefields of Troy that Homer describes. The gods inspire action rather than change objective circumstance. Akhilles, trapped in the waves of a river, is "not lifted above toil and struggle" but is inspired by the gods to overcome circumstance.

Yet sometimes, at certain moments of history, the gods themselves act. Athena guides the spear of Diomedes and Pandarus dies. Aphrodite carries Aeneas from the field of battle and certain death. At those moments of divine intervention, of course, the Greek and Trojan warriors are not aware of the presence of the gods. As Otto points out, outside of Homer's religious and poetic insight, the events of war are resolved into purely natural and familiar processes. Athena herself drives the spear of the warrior Diomedes, which his own hands thrust into the body of Ares. For Homer, man's highest deeds and heroic actions are the agency of the gods. Only a few of the chosen spiritual warriors see the divine manifestation. Other warriors know nothing and must speak of luck or the power of their own bodies as if it were "subjective" and innate. Apollo kicks down the wall of the Greeks, but remains invisible.

For Homer, the most admired prowess of the mightiest heroes must emphasize the presence of divinity. The bold, chosen warrior gathers up his gifts of mental wit and physical power and drives the ashen spear towards his enemy, but it is the wise Athena of the flashing eyes who guides the spear in action. The warrior's boldness, his physical strength at the significant moment of history, his ethical merit and cunning, were the gifts of the gods all along. The objective material spear itself was guided by the hands of deity.

I believe that this legacy of Homer, though not explicit in Plato's writing, is implicitly diffused throughout his thought. It is the understood context of his explicit teachings that take their meanings from the whole atmosphere of the Greek warrior cultus. This military ethos was founded on the poetic art of the blind Greek minstrel that Plato confesses he loved so much.

* * * * *

Plato's Republic exists only on paper. Because of this we will have to look elsewhere for real examples of military professionals who are developed after a Platonic model. I have already suggested that Crusaders like Tancred would fit the Platonic model quite well. I believe that it is in the historic roots of chivalry that we can best see an approximation of Plato's warrior class. An approximation, of course, is not an exact reproduction. Many moral, philosophical, and religious currents will join Plato's Greek thought by the time European knighthood has its opening on soil quite different from pre-Christian Athens.

I believe that the best historic example of Plato's warrior class might be found in southern France during the Middle Ages. It is here that the medieval renaissance of romanticism makes its initial flowering. It is a new kind of beauty in western civilization. Here in Provence and Languedoc, troubadour art and courtly love will form the zeitgeist which will produce the chivalric warrior. It is a unique event in western civilization and it is Platonic to its very heart. Courtesy, chivalry, and romantic love became the moral military drill of a new conception of the soldier. The art of the age exalted the fair knight, the skilled warrior, and the valorous soldier. Honor, love, and the joyous skill of life were its ideals. Here the ideal motif of manliness was the warrior, poet, and lover integrated in the balanced harmony of the knight. The Gallic society of Provence developed a moral code of high caliber. It was based on joy, honor, and the inspirational cult of the woman. As Karl Vossler has said, it was knighthood which raised women to a position of status in European culture.[24]

None of this refinement is found in the code of the northern European barbarian warrior. The heroes of the <u>Chansons de Gest</u> or the Icelandic sagas, live by a code of valor and death on the field of battle. That is all. As Christopher Dawson points out, "there is nothing save the name in common between the rude Christian chivalry of the north and the refined secular courtly chivalry of the south."

The key to the artistic refinement in medieval southern France lies in the mystical doctrine of Platonic love. This is best exemplified to some degree by the troubadour poetry of Arnaut Daniel with its intensive idealization of romantic love. It is a full blown Platonic idealism. Much of the early southern French ideas on romance, of course, is openly hedonistic. But it must be kept in mind that the very same culture which produced this troubadour tradition of knighthood was highly ascetic as well as aesthetic. The Manichean neo-Platonic dualism of the French cathars was considered extreme even by the strict standards of Latin Christianity.

This was especially true of sexual passion. Sensuality was put at the service of art, religion, and war. This all had its dark side, as all extremes do, and was eventually suffocated during the Albigensian crusade in the flames of war. But the warrior ideal of nobility, honor, and courtly love continued to live in the code of war and chivalry. The knight, like Beni 'Odhra's children of chastity, finds his power in Platonic love, the swordsman's skill, and the art of horsemanship. Gallantry and spiritual refinement become the soul of the new knightly orders, which come closest to what Plato had in mind over a thousand years earlier.

The knight is the paradigm of Plato's sacred warrior. In <u>King Arthur and the Grail</u>, Richard Cavendish analyzes the grail legends for their moral meaning.

He points out that the round table is an exalted military order. These knights are developed through a testing process. The knight-errant must measure himself against the odds of challenge and response. He loves adventures because that love is rooted in the deep need to stretch his nerve to the limit. He seeks to win the acclaim of his fellow knights and the courtly woman. To do this he must right wrong and protect the innocent and unfortunate. In doing the task of justice, however, he is seeking an objective beyond these activities. It is a quest, a search for a central good which can only be found in action and danger. He cannot remain in safety. He must be a seeker of risk. He must place himself at the call of fate and the threat of dishonor and death. He must face and defeat these dangers. He risks what he has for what he ought to be. What is it, we may ask, that he is seeking?

Richard Cavendish suggests that the knight-errant is seeking the true self, the perfect integrity of character, ". . .welded under the hammer-blows of danger." This character is a key to his immortality. It is gained only by valor. The knight cannot stay in a place of safety and pleasure. His true path is in the grave risks of earthly war. His staple occupation, the occupation of the Arthurian hero, is fighting. War, quests and sport (tournaments) are his activities. Fighting is the high road to personal integrity. He knows by spiritual insight that mind, nerve, muscle, courage, skill and experience are developed at the highest moments of human competition just as individual character is developed by historic process.

Richard Cavendish points out that these knights are not mere brutes, too unintelligent to feel fear or self-doubt. They are, in fact, high-strung, emotional and sensitive. They know fear in its most awful forms and must struggle to steel themselves against it. They can ". . .be knocked off their psychological balance as well as their horses." They weep in disappointment and defeat. After all, "A man who lives by stretching his nerves is likely to be a mass of nerves." His integrity, then, is achieved through struggle, conflict and self-mastery. Again, the medieval hero is sensitive to love and feminine beauty. A knight fights better when he is in love and his heroism is inspired by the flame of beauty as well as the flame of war. It is here, of course, that there is a subtle balance and even tension between the knight as a fighter and as a lover. If he is a slave of passion he is robbed of his integrity and honor, and even "of the possibility of true and lasting love." In mindless sensual pleasure, the knight loses his capacity for action. The encounter with the femme fatale is always a peril the true hero must experience and survive if he is to be a moral actor on the stage of history. These warriors must risk their ability to act, not in fleeing from feminine beauty, but in conquering themselves in love and chastity.

The knight's courage is tested by the stretching of nerve and prowess. He must pursue a goal he cannot see. Often he rides from the castles of safety to discover what the quest will be. He has no assurance of victory. He only knows that he must bear himself well whatever may happen. He is a seeker of danger for its own sake so that he can become his "finer self."

This round table is an elite band of men and women. Community is essential to knightly development. In moments of crisis, however, the hero is called to act alone. The warrior must face danger ". . .by himself, with only himself to rely on, for only so can he find himself." For the hero, lonely courage is the mark of the noble champion. The uncanny forest, the enchanted castle, the perilous chapel, the enticing garden with its lovely fay enchantresses, are all challenges, gauntlets thrown at the feet of the hero who must master both his natural sensuousness and the force of the supernatural. He will face the ultimate temptation of a refuge filled with a dream-land full of romantic loves in opposition to the hard and brutal road of duty and danger.

The calls to purity, austerity, simplicity, disciplined dedication and chastity will come into powerful conflict with the knight's natural love of safety and high strung awareness of pleasure. None of the knights will be untried or unscathed in these conflicts. Most will have moments of doubt, many will reel from stark moral failure. Cowardice and sensuality will fell most of them at times. But the best will overcome and pursue, against great odds, not only the external foes of justice but the more terrible internal foes that strike at the very heart of right action.

This view of the world, Cavendish points out, is individualistic and aristocratic. Evil, in these stories, controls its slaves for years. Society is helpless before the power of dragons or evil knights. They can only wait for the arrival of a hero, one who may have to overcome his instincts of pity, self-doubt, and his moral awareness of the chaos which might result from his action.

This is not only the affirmation of the warrior ethos of southern France, but fits well into the whole concept of Plato's warrior class.

Growth takes place in risk. In the face of danger, normal securities evaporate for the mythic knight. The dragon can be psychologically overpowering. The knight seeks the dragon not because he is brave but so that he can become brave. It is his fear which is conquered rather than the dragon. The rebuke of evil is the whetstone upon which his character is sharpened. If the knight is to be successful in the quest, there will always be the internal victory of a spiritual nature before there is an external conquest. The key, in the grail legends, lies in the realm of divine power. It is confession and prayer, fasting and religious ritual, ordination and forgiveness, which are the means of success. No knight's nerve will hold against the sudden presence of the dragon unless he is empowered by divine spirit. If he sells his power for forbidden pleasure, he loses his moral cohesiveness. If he stays in the secret garden of pleasure instead of pursuing his quests, he loses his moral congruency. Though the knight may act alone, he is developed in the sacraments of religious community. Monk, priest, wise women of the forests and church, create the necessary environment for knighthood. Prayer, fasting, and religious service work within the structure of religious community. This is the preparation which ends when the hero rides forth to act so that he can be. Risk and danger at the call of justice are the test as well as the teacher of knighthood.

Out of the processes and testing grounds, the moral psychology of knighthood is developed. In all things, pressure is the fountainhead of power and danger is the forge of character. This European knight in the fullest sense is a morally refined military professional. It is not the berserker fury of the Norseman with his cult of blood and death, nor even the Homeric hero seeking the glory of battle. It is instead a code of gentleness, service, and humility, which in a flash becomes resolve and boldness motivated by a refining love in the face of danger. Here is our Platonic watchdog in its most supreme form. The Norman knight would be a type. Here the Norse warrior cultus of battle is civilized by the Judeo-Christian culture. The metamorphosis produces the crusader whose roots reach all the way back to a young poet and wrestler who one day met Socrates and so began to change the soul of western culture.

* * * * *

The emphasis on the close connection between physical discipline and spiritual training is central to the Indian religious heritage, Buddhist, Jain, and Hindu. The extensive and ancient varieties of yoga were transmitted by Indian Buddhist monks to China, where Zen (Ch'an) training became central to much of Chinese and Japanese religion. This Zen or transmitted yoga was both athletic and meditative. Religious training was soon turned to military development, especially at the Shaolin Monastery, the original center of martial arts training.

Zen eventually became the molding force, not only of the Chinese arts of empty hand fighting but of the Japanese Samurai military tradition. The religious training of monks had, as a consequence, produced a military class. The perfect mirror of wisdom (daien-kyochi), enlightenment (tensho and samadhi, both positive and absolute) , thought impulse (nen and ichi-nen) , self-mastered enlightened quality (jishu-zammai), the koan, and zazen postures became so many tools for the development of martial power. In Noh acting, judo, and kendo, respiration and tanden (abdominal) control came out of the religious disciplines of Indian Buddhist communities, themselves routed in ancient Indian yogas. Act, or acting, was a religious point of initiation into being.

For the Indian disciplines, what is true for organic nature is also true for inorganic nature. Spirit is developed by spiritual discipline, character by the disciplined decision of act. A lord of war and a lord of spirit are made in the same way. A knight becomes brave if, and only if, he faces the terrifying, first by a sheer act of will, and then by self-conquest in the major dimensions of his interior life. Character creates the new self.

In the quarterly Philosophy East and West, October, 1981, Shigenori Nagatomo analyzes the training concepts of Zemi, the 14th century Zen master. Zeami is interested in the development of acting skill for a Japanese Noh drama. Zeami proposes that the actor must first learn to imitate. He begins by putting his body into a certain form, itself an ideal pattern. One does not learn a martial art, for instance, by intellectually theorizing but by doing the punch or kick. Will trains the mind through the body. As the disciple imitates an acting pattern, he undergoes a transformation. He brings to his character a celestial addition. As he subjects himself to rigorous training, he will "own what is imitated." He becomes the imitated pattern. By going through the bodily modalities the actor becomes that nature. To act "like a tiger" is to become like a tiger. These acquisitions of personality traits in Japanese drama come out of the performer's techniques. There is a structured and progressive ascent of appropriation. The point here is that this becoming is first initiated through physical action. Our self is not just "mind" with a "body" as an instrument. Drawing on Zen tradition, Zeami points out that we correct our mode of consciousness by assuming bodily form (as in seated meditation) or in activities like dance, sport, or religious liturgy. Thus ". . . the respective status of our mind and body is equal, existentially as well as axiologically." The use of physical activity is a restoration of "primordial identity." Movement becomes independent from "striving consciousness" as the body becomes a true initiator of action.

The body-mind action is done without thinking. The actor, by acting, has appropriated nature. Freedom of will, then, is an achieved quality. It is achieved by giving the body precedence over one's mind. One's power of freedom of will is a process of degrees. By imposing a physical discipline on one' s body, one actualizes freedom in a process of training. According to this view, the "true self" of a person is the result of any given activity of appropriation at the time of imitative training. It is, in Zeami's thought, an embodiment and expression of freedom of action, as well as that of mind. More important, this freedom, to be what is imitated, cannot be achieved by intellectual understanding, but only through imitation. The "true self" is to be attained by a correcting of consciousness through imposing a discipline of body into a "form," a way of being, either by Zen meditation or martial arts.

This type of Zen philosophy used in Japanese drama has a correspondence with Plato's thought in the development of a Greek warrior. The initial educational process in Book III and IV of the Republic emphasizes character development through willed and imposed habit. In the exercise of the body in Greek sport, there is a yoga which is Zen in nature. Sport imposes grace in motion. The testing of the initiate's character requires decision and the exercise of the will. In Plato, unlike the Shaolin monastic tradition, Greek sport, though it has a religious dimension, does not have the formal meditative component of Indian spiritual training. Greek sport, from Homeric times, was thought of as a type of religious celebration or ceremony. Yet, in comparison to an athletic discipline like Indian Hatha yoga or the Shaolin meditative system of Boddhi-Dharma, Greek sport is more social and humanistic in tone. We are not, however, to ignore Plato's emphasis on the absoluteness of the transcendent in his transformational notions of education. For Plato, understanding is more important than yoga or meditative techniques. The eventual power of the Macedonian phalanx did not come from the religious practices of Indian religion.

Zeami's concept of imitation has a more profound parallel in Plato's philosophy of art and character. For Plato, art imprints moral values on the mind of the potential auxiliary. For Plato, only literature which gives a correct view of the goodness and justice of God should be used in educating the young. We have "a good and bad part" in our soul (Rep. 431-A). One must be especially careful of "a new form of music" (poetry) as "a universal danger" (Rep. 424-C). Art "gently flows into people's dispositions and pursuits . . . then, raging with depravity, sweeps down on laws and constitutions" (Rep. 424-E). "The most sovereign nature lies in poetry" (music) because "its rhythms and melodies enter the innermost part of the soul" (Rep 401-E). At times Plato seems to give up on art and dismiss it as simple eikasia (conjecture) or the lowest form of learning. But he wants his future political, philosophic, and military lords to be taught a literature which is heroic in its very core. The initiate is educated in this literature for the very purpose of imitating the heroic role models presented to him from his earliest childhood. This is not formal Eastern meditation but it is a powerful artistic development of the imagination which is guided toward a warrior ethos.

By listening to these heroic myths, the future Greek warriors, male and female, will have their souls imprinted with the seeds of virtue and valor. In the Zen metaphor of Zeami, to hear about the tiger is to be inspired to act like the tiger. In Plato's sequence, we first hear, then do. Art becomes inspiration. By trying to imitate the hero, we become the hero. Like the imitation in Noh drama, the warrior, after being inspired by the stories of valor, must act like the hero until it becomes habit, a spontaneous second nature. This transformation calls down the celestial addition, and the soul is disciplined and formed after the ideal pattern of martial character, not by Eastern yoga but by Western art.

* * * * *

Finally, we must sum up the Platonic nature of the warrior. I have suggested that we can find an "extended" Plato in some forms of the neo-Platonic tradition. This I believe to be especially true about Plato's vision of the archetypical warrior. The Platonic warrior ethos may find its most mature paradigm in Plotinus. In The Enneads, Plotinus argued that the good society was a society of valor. Evil, he says, can only triumph because of the moral feebleness on the part of the defeated. "Bad men rule by the feebleness of the ruled." God ordains that this must be so, for "the triumph of weaklings would not be just." Why complain, he said if "... the ignoble" get a "richer harvest if they are the only workers in the fields." Plotinus puts it in a most blunt and provocative way. "Not even a god would strike a blow for the unwarlike." It is ordained by God that "... the duly armed" will win the battle. With a bemused scorn he describes a gang of Roman youths, "... morally negligent ... but in good physical training," stealing food and clothes from those who have not trained either "physically or morally." The victims suffer "the penalty of their sloth and self-indulgence." They did "... not arm themselves" and it is "... the duly armed who win the day."

Plotinus argues that the world separated from the divine justice is governed by force. The inactive must suffer needless injustice. Using a metaphor both Shakespearean and Indian in its tone, Plotinus compares the world to a play. Each soldier must act his part, play well the role assigned to him. Victory is possible only to those who fight well, not to those who simply pray. Prayer without action cannot be victorious in a world ruled by greed and force. Pride, lust, and terror must be met by the warrior trained in the divine ideas and the vision of spiritual realities. The moral life of the warrior must be directed toward "The One," God, the mystic center of the cosmos and the individual soul. Like Plato, Plotinus describes the divine knight as one who knows two worlds at once: the divine realities and the world of war and action. Power is grounded in a religious vision which subsumes the world of pain and death under the reality of ultimate ends, values, and meanings. Plotinus warns prospective warriors that they are not to allow themselves to be pushed from their positions assigned them by fate but to stand firm and fight knowing that it is all a play, but a play of vital, spiritual importance.

Here it is not meditation but contemplation of the ideals which is essential. One does not rely on a disciplined formal yoga but on The One. Plotinus would stress the pure simplicity of prayer to the Gods of Fate and the straightforward action of war in a just cause.

We may conclude, then, that Plato's warrior ethos is founded on a religious and philosophic humanism which avoids two possible errors. He is not interested in the creation of a technically proficient military professional with no real values. Neither does he wish to produce a warrior who in the name of a false spirituality or moral sensitivity cannot meet the contingencies of combat. Instead he proposes the development of a warrior ethos grounded on the life of the spirit, the life of reason and the hard mastery of the self and the weapons of war.▲

How is Plato's concept of the Good, that which is beyond being, to be understood? For Plat the Good has nothing directly to do with philosophy as a conventional understanding. It is better to see this aspect of Plato's thought as mystical and religious. Socrates was first and foremost an ecstatic, a visionary (*Symp.* 174d-175c). It is the connection of the soul with the logos which is of importance to the Socratic teaching (*Phaed.* 67c, 80e, 83a-c). As E. R. Dodds points out, God works directly on the emotional life through the inspired poets drawing humans like a magnet (*Laws* 536a). This description of divine activity is religious and mystical in its very essence.25 It is a concept of a return to a forgotten light which give a spiritual meaning to human existence. This return, however, is revelatory in its inspiration. The light draws us and this drawing is at the same time an empowerment for actions which create the nature of our character. E. R. Dodds describes Plato's guardians "as a new kind of rationalized shamans" who are trained for earthly activity "by a special kind of discipline designed to modify the whole psychic structure." It is the exaltation of the daimonios man and woman (*Rep.* 468e). He can talk of God, the gods, or the good with equal ease. more than any other philosopher he uses the language of myth, religion, and metaphysics to convey the same crucial spiritual meaning for human existence. Above all, he first points to the religious dimension in the human soul for the unifying factor, and then upward to the divine for vision and power.

It is this religious approach which distinguishes Plato from so many other philosophers. It is his evocative pointing to a spiritual center which transforms mere intellectual pursuit into a true soteriological discipline. In his novel Till We Have Faces C.S. Lewis posits the clear difference between a religious view of life and the tasks of moral philosophy.

"The Fox," a Greek stoic captured in war, is taunted by "the Priest" before the King's court. This Greek wisdom, the Priest says, "brings no corn; sacrifice does both." the stoic philosophy of the Fox, "does not give them boldness to die." It was in war that "he threw down his arms and let them bind his hands and lead him away and sell him, rather than take a spear thrust in his heart." His philosophy doesn't even give him an "understanding of holy things." This philosopher demands to "see such things clearly as if the gods were no more than letters written in a book. Nothing that is said clearly can be said truly about them. Holy places are dark places. It is life and strength, not knowledge and words, that we get in them. Holy wisdom is not clear and thin like water, but thick and dark like blood." From this perspective the Platonic warrior training is not so much a philosophical pursuit as an ascetic discipline of sacrifice and religious ritual which brings the power of the gods to the individual soul. As Orual, the lead character in the novel, watches the Fox and the Priest "it was easy to see which side the strength lay."

This religious perspective seems to fit in well with much that Plato believes. Can we say that moral training does not make spiritual power but is the occasion for the emanation of spiritual strength? Here we must look for a concept of Platonic religious inspiration (in-spiriting) as an act of grace. In the Ion Socrates argues that true poetic art occurs as an ecstatic experience. Here Poetry is a gift of the gods. The poets are "taken out of themselves." They are like seers or bacchanals. He Plato makes a direct comparison between artistic inspiration and religious inspiration. both types of inspiration come from divinity to the individual. In the end of the Symposium (Symp. 223d), Socrates argues that artists are instruments of a genius which masters them. It should be kept in mind that it is Socrates himself who is mastered by one of his "raptures" at the start of the dialogue.

In the Phaedrus (244a-256e) Socrates argues that ecstasy or inspired "exaltation" like prophecy is a divine activity. the ecstasy of purifications and initiations is also a type of transcendent inspiration like poetry and love. Is Plato arguing for the logical priority of divine inspiration in poetry, love, religion, or the Socratic philosophical development and knowledge upon which society and the warrior class are based?

In the Politics Plato seems to reject the passionless objectivity of the philosopher kings for a more passionate participation in human affairs (Pol. 297d-e). As Dodds points out, the virtue of the common man is not simple knowledge of the Good by a process of moral training (Laws 6536) by "incantations."26 It involves a purging of the "folly of the body" in ethical warfare. It was G.M.A. Grube in his Plato's Thought, who pointed out the significance of the directing of the passions toward action and knowledge in Plato (Rep. 485d) "as though the stream had been diverted there." The "terrible and indispensable passions" (Tim. 69c) must be harnessed and used (not repressed) for higher ends. For this, man must be made ready by religious ritual, music and dance. (Laws 803b-804b).27 Man must be God's property (Laws 902b). He must bow and adore (Laws 716a). here it is Plato's genuine religious thought which is to be distinguished from the occult magic falsehoods of augury and hepatoscopy (Phaed. 244c-d). it is not magic power he is after but the spiritual power grounded in the Good. It "is to think rightly about the gods and so live well" (Laws 888b).

Finally, Plato's very personalized religious vision about the universe is described most clearly in his concept of the world forming process. God, deciding "to form the world in the closest likeness to the most beautiful of intelligible beings and to a Being perfect in all things, made into a living being, one visible, and having within itself all living beings of like nature with itself" (Tim. 30d 2-5). The Platonic warrior whose soul is trained be a religious vision is to defend a universe described through that religion.

In Plato's thought we can see the elements of a religious vision that produced a culture of unsurpassed military heros. It is strange that in our own day the discussion of a warrior ethos is quite often framed around the motif of the samurai tradition. the spiritual dimensions of the warrior class are usually seen in the context of Eastern thought; Chinese, Japanese or Indian. The Western spiritual tradition is normally not seen as hawing any connection with a warrior ethos.

Spirit

The Greek, Roman, Judaic, Islamic and Christian religious systems seem divorced from the development of fighting personnel. This is strange in the light of the facts of military history. Certainly an arguable good case can be made that the Western military tradition developed out of the Western religions and philosophical systems is superior to the Eastern military tradition. (See this thesis more maturely developed in my book *Winning Wars, the Spiritual Dimension in Military Art*, University Press of America, 1986.) The Zen samurai warrior ethos is overemphasized by those who, in Karl Jung's words "have let there own temples become overgrown with weeds and now wish to break into the temples of others." ▲

In Book 8, beginning with 559d of the <u>Republic</u>, Plato describes youth raised in a democracy. They are beguiled by "colorful pleasures" that drive them "in every direction." They grant liberty and license (to) useless, "unnecessary pleasures." These youth live "from day to day gratifying whatever desire happens to turn up. They even pretend to "dabble in philosophy" and "politics." There is "no order or necessity in (their) life." It is a life of disorder that is "blissful, free, and pleasant." One hears continually of "freedom" and "equal rights." But these slogans are only a mask to disobey their rulers, teachers, and parents. Fathers act "like their children." The old condescend to the young" and students hold their teachers in contempt." "Mob liberty" culminates in a city "like this," Plato says. His jubilant exaggeration extends to the description of the dogs in a democracy "behaving like the proverbial masters." Even "the very horses and mules" are "bristling with freedom" and equality. The souls of these citizens are, of course, "too sensitive" to endure hardship. Because of "democracy's permissiveness," violent changes go to excess. Plato pictures this moral corruption as a "desire" that acts like "bile and phlegm" in the body. Culture is led by stingless drones, "that class of lazy, spendthrift men, led by the brave, followed by the cowardly." In a democracy, Plato says, "this is the dominant class." Such a society educates its young not in the warrior ethos but in a liberal relativity of the sophists that saps all virtue and, therefore, all virility. This is certainly a devastating attack on democracy.

It must be kept in mind, however, that Plato is describing a certain type of democracy in Athens at a specific period in its history. He knew as well as anyone in Greece that democracies could produce, and had produced, a military class of citizens that defeated the overwhelming numbers of the Persian Empire. Athens herself had contributed most significantly to those stunning military upsets.

His observations of the democratic youth, then, are a warning of a significant shift in the moral center of a democratic city that educates its youth in a way that enervates their souls . Such youth would make poor soldiers. Plato had seen the youth of Sparta, still raised on the Dorian warrior code, defeat the youth of Athens educated in the pleasures of the Athenian party life, of which Alcibiades was a supreme example.

What would Plato think of American democracy and its ability to produce a successfully military class? One can only speculate, but some observations might be made. Plato might think that education in liberal Western democracies could undermine those very qualities which are most important for the development of Plato's ideal warrior class. An exaggerated emphasis on ethical and cultural relativity (Protagoras' "man is the measure of all things") leaves no values that are worth dying for. Plato's objection to Athenian democracy is not that people can vote for their rulers. In the <u>Laws</u>, Plato mandates the voting rights of the populous. Guardians are voted into office. Plato is objecting to the relativistic moral climate of Athens and its consequent effect on the souls of the young. If all values are equal, what justification is there in defending one set of cultural norms (say democracy itself) over another set (say the totalitarian state)?

Older democracies, unlike young democracies, may have a natural tendency toward relativism and egalitarianism. The effect on the youth in older democracies could seem to conform to the descriptive picture Plato paints of the youth of Athens. Older democracies can produce a youth cult as a predominant fashion. The soul of such cultures is easily convulsed by fad and the assertiveness of the most shrill. The centers of moral, religious, and artistic norms dissolve into the whims of subjectivity. One will die for kith, kin, and kind, God and fatherland, but would one die for the normless? A warrior code takes root in the virtue of sacrifice. The risk of death, the possibilities of maiming, are not sought after by the seeker of comfort and pleasure. War in just defense of one's values demands ultimate sacrifices. Discipline and the postponement of gratification cannot take root in cultures which stress unlimited pleasures. Heroic values dissolve in the face of an education which emphasizes the "odyssey of the self-centered self." Such cultures must unconsciously begin to develop an internal self-hatred. Who would die to perpetuate such an unheroic mess? "

Such a mass is easily victimized by those who know how to use force and are committed to something, however horrible. A democracy sliding into senility will be very squeamish about using force. Intimidated by the power of others which threatens their pleasures, they do not wish to use force which would require sacrifices on the part of their citizens. Such cultures hire mercenaries, either from foreign countries or from the class of the economic underprivileged, so that the middle class can continue its drive for material comfort. Such cultures rarely produce the elemental force of a Bohemund or the refinement of a St. Benedict. These things, of course, go by degrees in the dialectical shifts of history and the times. The moral state of American democratic youth may be hard to determine in moral setting that mixes iron and clay.

The teenage community of ancient Sparta, of course, was raised in a quite different moral atmosphere. Here, loyalty, initiative, brotherhood, and sisterhood were molded by the discipline of the Dorian warrior ethos. It had its dark side and its eventual sexual degeneracy, but at its best, it produced a quiet (laconic) stability of character, an independence and self-possession lacking in the youth of Athens. For Plato, the political problem was to find the right means of combining the freedoms of Greek democracy with the necessary moral disciplines that mold the interior life of its citizenry.

We might see Plato's ideal in another type of culture. The forest and plains Indian culture is an excellent example of the molding power of a warrior ethos. The emphasis on self-possession, silence, and action created a climate of moral discipline in which martial ardor could flourish. Here, the warrior and the martyr, one who fights against impossible odds, could be combined. Not the avoidance of death but the fulfillment of honor became the chief end of this chivalry. The warrior lodges of tribal society produced a marvelous young military with an overriding nobility. Plato would probably be more impressed with the warriors of the Cheyenne "Dog Soldier" society than with major segments of the Western campus — its lack of moral challenge and its lack of religious initiation. The plains Indian youth were molded by prayer, fasting, and austerities. It is these qualities which would probably attract most of Plato's admiration.

These warrior qualities of the American Indians in no way lessened the strong individualism and independent nature of the cult of action. In ancient Sparta, individual initiative was developed to a high degree. The young Spartan male was sent into the hills alone for months on his "walk about." This same individualism was present to the hunting society of the American Indian. Solitude and communion were stressed and developed. Here are examples that the warrior ethos is not detrimental to individuality and its consequent democratic process.

For Plato, of course, the warrior ethos is part of the journey of the soul, a mystic way, of amor ascendens, in which the eventual end is to "lose itself in light." In A. E. Taylor's German "der Mensch ist etwas das uberwunden werden muss," we only become fully human as we become something more. In all of this, the divine is central. For Plato, the spiritual state of the soul is the central force of military action and the quest of philosophy. Here the saint, the knight, and the visionary guardian merge in a mosaic of high action. At the call of justice this type of person is best fitted to serve the lords of war.

Those interested in an analysis of Tolkien's characters might consult Randel Helms' Tolkien's World (Houghton Mifflin Company, 1974), especially chapters III and IV. For those interested in the Zen influence on the Japanese military tradition see Stephen Turnbull's comments in his interesting book The Samurai: A Military History (Macmillan, 1977). Check Mercea Eliade's Patanjali and Yoga (Schocken Books, 1975) for an interesting commentary on Patanjali's thought and concepts on spiritual discipline. Also see How to Know God, (Vedanta Press, 1953), Prabhavananda and Isherwood. A typical example of health from a Hatha Yogic standpoint can be seen in yogi Ramacharaka's Hatha Yoga (D.B. Taraporevala Sons and Co., private LTD., Bombay, 1966). these types of books are traditional stock-in-trade in India. See Charles Williams' Descent of the Dove and Theology (Wm. B. Eerdmans Co.) for his thoughts on attitude and spirituality. He may be the most esoteric neo-Platonic writer in 20th century literature. Evelyn Underhill's book Practical Mysticism (E.P. Dutton, 1915) stresses the importance of the spiritual path for average practical persons like Florence Nightengale or modern soldiers like General Gordon. It is a well worth consluting–brief and simple. for a deeper study on neo-Platonic mysticism see her classic work, Mysticism. See Aristotle's Ethics (in the Basic Works of Aristotle, Random House, 1941) pages 935-1111 for a full development of his though on virtue. For those interested in Arthurian romance King Arthur and His Knight of the Round Table (Penguin Books, 1953) by Roger Lancelyn Green is the best modern work for the uninitiated. Maybe William Buck's loosely paraphrased translation of Valmki's Ramayan (Mentor Books, New American Library, 1976) is best for the western beginner interest in Rama as hero. for scholars interested in the pursuit of moral notions in Chines Confucian thought like "jen" or "li" see A.S. Cua's short but provocative article in Journal of Chinese Philosophy Volume 6, no. 1, March 1979, pages 55-56. See especially his very brief attempt to compare "jen" and "agape." See Xenophon's The Persian Expedition (The Penguin Classics, trans. by Rex Warner, 1949) for the full account of a highly successful military retreat and the fiber of the Greek warrior. For a liberal popularized view of Asian sexual practice see Sexual Secrets (Destiny Books, 1979) by Douglas and Slinger. It represents a minority viewpoint of more radical tantric practice. Those interested in a contemporary conservative commentary on Patanjali's thought can consult Rammurti S. Mishra's Yoga Sutras The Text Book of Yoga Philosophy, (Anchor Books, 1973). See especially pages 137-138, 196-198. Older histories tend to emphasize the ideal aspects of Greek thought. See for instance Charles Rollin's, The Ancient History of the Egyptians, Carthaginians, Assyrians, Babylonians, Medes and Persians, Macedonians and Grecians (John Wurtele Lovell, no date, 4 vol.). See volume I on Greek character development. for an interesting 20th century defense of moderate continence as a base of Romantic love see Marie Stopes" Married Love (Eugenics Publishing Company, Inc., 1935). One hardly hears of it now even though such an authority as Havelock Ellis was impressed by her thinking. It is highly influenced by a victorian Platonism. See

Thucydides' <u>The Peloponnesian War</u> *(Penguin Classics, 1956) on page 51 for accounts of Greek warfare. For an excellent and interesting development of aspects of the thought of Plotinus, see J.M. Rist's* <u>Plotinus, The Road to Reality</u> *(Cambridge University Press, 1967) especially on the connection between prayer and action on pages 199-212. on the whole issue of detachment see Robert C. Neville's* <u>Soldier, Sage, Saint</u> *(Fordham University Press, 1978) especially pages 39-42. Ramanuja's dialectical skill is brilliantly displayed in the* <u>Vedarsamgraha</u> *(Sr. Ramakrishna Ashrama, 1956, Mysore, India).28 See pages 18, 38, 137 for some examples. On the subject of prayer, Plotinus, in the Ennead 3.5.6 discusses the interesting concept of the "Spirit Guide" and prayer. See Christian Jochim's article on Chinese ethics in* <u>Philosophy East and West</u>, *April 1981, especially his analysis of "chi" in the* <u>Mencius</u> *on page 170, for a comparison of "rightness" and religious experience with Plato's conception of justice. for an interesting and profound study of the whole area of human conceptual thought and reality see K. Venkata Ramana's tightly written exploration of Nagarjuna's epistemology in* <u>Nagarjuna's Philosophy</u> *(Samuel Weiser, Inc., 1966). See especially pages 111-126. for a significantly modified ethical perspective on the issue of justified homicide see Ramchandra Gandhi's article "On Meriting Death" in the quarterly* <u>Philosophy East and West</u>, *July, 1981, pages 337-353. He argues in an interesting and sensitive way that no one ever has a right to take life but some may have the duty to take life. does he see that we have a right to do a duty, or, better yet, that duty categorically confers moral right? Does his abhorrence of violence obscure his moral insight? He is not a pacifist, however, and one wonders if a truly universal pacifist position is ever ethically defensible in any philosophical description.*

Aristotle's <u>Ethics</u> *(Everyman's Library, Dutton New York, 1963) is his most provocative writing on the Hindu view of war and society. E.J. Urwick's* <u>The Platonic Quest</u> *is an interesting attempt at describing the parallels between Indian thought and Plato. (it is published by Concord Grove Press, London, 1983.)*

For those interested in Tibetan religion or Madhyamika Buddhist thought, K Venkata Ramanan's <u>Nagarjuna's Philosophy</u> *(Samuel Weiser, Inc., New York, 1966), is the most concise and lucid account in the English language. For the well-written condensed summary of the German romanticist like Schelling, see* <u>From Descartes to Wittgenstein</u>, *by Roger Scruton, (Harper Colophon Books, New York, 1981), pp.162-164. for a most provocative description of Platonic philosophy see Paul Friedländer's* <u>Plato, An Introduction</u> *(Bollingen Series LIX-1l, Princeton, 1958). I am deeply indebted to A.E. Taylor's* <u>Plato, The Man and His Work</u> *(Meridian Books, New York, 1957).* <u>Medieval Essays</u>, *by Christopher Dawson (Image Books, Doubleday, 1959), was a great stimulus to my thoughts about chivalry. He puts a greater stress on the separation between the knightly code of southern France and the Christian tradition than may be warranted. He argues very persuasively that the warrior ethos of Languedoc was Islamic in nature if not in origin. However, he and I both see the influence of Platonic idealism (see p. 209). Again, he denies any direct connection between the troubadour tradition and the Albigenses while I am more agnostice (see p. 206).*

John Kenneth Atchity's <u>Homer's Illiad, The Shield of Memory</u> (Southern Illinois University Press, Carbondale, 1978) is still the best description of Homer's warrior code in print. Richard Cavendish's literary exposition of the moral meanings in Arthurian Romance is highly readable and worthwhile (<u>King Arthur and the Grail</u>, Paladin, Grandada Publishing Limited, London, 1980). For those interested in a provocative defense of the Greek religious ideals, <u>The Homeric Gods</u> (Thames and Hudson, 1979) by Walter Otto is worth serious study. He sees Greek religion as separate and superior to the new religions of the western world whereas I see them as more complementary. For those interested in Plotinus and a neo-Platonic philosophy of religious vision and war see my <u>Winning Wars, The Spiritual Dimension in Military Art</u>, (University Press of America, 1986).▲

FOOTNOTES

1. See E. R. Dodds provocative essay in Vlastos' Plato, II, Ethics, Politics and Philosophy of Art and Religion. Doubleday Anchor Original, N.Y. , 1971, where he argues that "The identification of the detachable 'occult self' " from the "psyche" involved "a complete re-interpretation of the old Shamanistic culture-patterns" (p. 209). It is at this point that philosophy distinguishes itself from the occult.

2. See the Republic 486A where Plato argues that we are not to be simple, unemotional "spectators" of human existence. In the Laws 663B, he argues "for action which brings more joy than sorrow." This is a rationalism, Dodds says (p. 212, ibid.) that is "quickened with ideas that once were magical." Here the emergence of reason over spiritualism does not negate the life of passion and involvement.

3. The nous is central to Plato's epistemology. The nous is the purest part of reason, free from the irrational impositions of the mingling of body and soul. See Paul Friedländer's Plato, An Introduction, Bolliner Series, Princeton, 1958, p. 37. It may also be interesting to compare Plato's use of the word nous with the Sanskrit terms buddhi (higher faculty of moral judgment) or adyatmavidya (pure knowledge of reality).

4. Anamnesis is a soul memory akin in some ways to Carl Jung's collective unconscious. In Indian thought, the remembrance of past moral experiences is a preparation for anasakti (pure, unselfish action). See Raghavanlyer's Essay in E. J. Urwick's The Platonic Quest, Concord Grove Press, 1983.

5. Plato seems to have gone beyond the Socratic dictum that no one knowingly does wrong. For Plato, moral evil is more than a simple intellectual error. The divine and sinless soul is made not simply by philosophic training but through "purgation." He seemed to believe that there was an unaccountable, irrational factor in the soul itself. See the Timaeus 89E and the Laws 896D, as well as G. M. Grube's Plato's Thought, 129-149. Dodd proposes that Plato, in the Sophist, argues for "a disease of the soul" (p. 214, ibid.).

6. This moral balance is the fons et origo of all intelligence. By developing a moral nature, we become susceptible to a higher reality. In Schelling's idealism, the relationship between the divine infinite and the finite is the chief problem of philosophy. (See pp. 94-148 in Volume Three of Copleston's A History of Philosophy, Image Books 1965, 67, 77 for a summary of Schelling's thought.) For Plato, sophrosyne is a preparation for this unity.

7. The concept of a military brotherhood was probably derived by Socrates from the aristocratic culture of the Doric warriors. See Paul Friedländer's ideas on p. 44 of his Plato, An Introduction.

8. This is Aeschines Socraticus. See A. E. Taylor's Plato, the Man and His Work, p. 133.

9.   Aspasia, according to Aeschines, was a woman of high political ability and Rhodogyne was an Amazon queen. A. E. Taylor, Plato, The Man and His Work. p. 133 believes that Plato is influenced in his attitude toward women by these women warrior models. I tend to lean toward Crete and Sparta as historical influences.

10.   See Srimat Swami Shivananda Saraswati's Yogic Byaym for Students, Brahmachri Yogashram 471 Netaji Colony, Calcutta, 1978, pp. 198-202.

11.   For those interested in Shankaras' philosophy, see The Vedanta Sutras of Badaravana and Shankaras' commentary, Dover Publications, Inc. , N.Y. , N.Y., 2 vol., 1962.

12.   Compare this type of description with the concept of "The feeling of presence" (sentiment de presence) of M. Henri Delacroix. See Studies in the Psychology of the Mystics, Joseph Marechal, S. J., Magi Books, Inc., Albany, N.Y. , 1964, pp. 57-61. This feeling is more like a state of being than an emotion.

13.   See Paul Friedländer's chapter 3 on "Beyond Being" for a comparison of Plato with Eckhart, Pascal, Suso, Tauler, and Mechthild in his Plato, An Introduction, Bollinger Series, Princeton, 1958, especially pp. 71-84.

14.   In India, there is a distinction between left-hand Tantra (vamachara) and right-hand Tantra (bakshinachara). It is right-hand Tantra which emphasizes Platonic chastity. According to this Tantric view, celibacy (brahmacharya) creates an "upward flow" (urdhvaretas) of spiritual power (ojas-shakti). This power is the essence of manhood (virya) . For an esoteric view of human sexuality, See Julius Evola's The Metaphysics of Sex, Inner-traditions International, N.Y., 1983. I think his provocative views are marred by his somewhat occultish bent toward left-hand Tantra. Right-hand Tantra stresses a type of "sacred" chastity which integrates the natural forces of a warrior, a doctrine taught in the classic Indian text of the Mahabharata. (See C. Rajagopalchari's Mahabharata, Bharatiya Yidya Bhavan, Bombay, 1985.

In The Bhagavad-Gita, the warrior-hero Arjuna is told that "He whom thou will slay is already slain in me; be thou only the instrument." Julius Evola wonders if this "warrior heroism" is one of Plato's forms of (religious) "intoxication" (See p. 109). In India, the warrior must possess "suadharma" or loyalty to his warrior code. This is to be combined with the battle fury which disregards either victory or defeat but emphasizes simple duty.

15.   See Ajanta, Mulk Raj Anand, Marg Publications, McGraw.Hill, Bombay, 1971,and Illustrated Guild, Aurangabad, Dalltabad,EIlora, and Ajanta, Jayna Pub. Co., Delhi (text by umedra Verma) .

16.   Not that the Indian system is essentially impersonal; Shankara speaks of "isvara" the Lord as a personal god but only on the level of myth or illusion. Indian personalism is better represented by the yoga master Pantanjali who emphasized a personal lord and god for yoga initiates. See Pantajali's Yoga

Sutras for his full view of theistic personalism. For another viewpoint, see Vedanta for Modern Man, edited by Christopher Isherwood, Mentor Book, 1951, pp. 113-120.

17. It is interesting to compare the Greek concept of "eudaemonia" with the Indian concept of "bhakti" or "makarea." Is the "bliss" or "blessedness" of the mystical experience a feeling or a more integrated state of being? See W. R. Inge's Christian Mysticism, Living Age Books, Meridian, 1956, Lecture III, pp. 77, 122 for a provocative study of Platonic mysticism. Plato seems to argue for a mysticism of transformation rather than ecstasy. For Plato, character is superior to mystical phenomenon.

18. In The Platonic Quest, Concord Grove Press, 1983, E.J. Urwick argues for an understanding of Plato in traditional Indian terms. He argues that "adyatmavidy" (knowledge of reality) is best done by knowing the "atman" the eternal godhead within. See pp. 159-164. This may exaggerate the Eastern tone in Plato's Greek thought.

19. See Joseph Campbell's The Hero With a Thousand Faces, Bollinger Series, Princeton, 1949, especially pp. 49-58.

20. See M. D. Chenu's Nature, Man and Society in the Twentieth Century, University of Chicago, 1957. He speaks of the "Golden Age of Platonism" at the French School of Chartres. His exploration of the "imago Dei" in Platonic terms is insightful. (See p. 30 for his comments on the influence of the Timaeus on Western thought.)

21. It is interesting to compare Aristotle's concept of the citizen soldier with Machiavelli's statement in the Discorsi, that it is not "gold but good soldiers" that win wars. See Edward Mead Earle, Makers of Modern Strategy, Princeton, 1971, especially pp. 12.16.

22. See Arnold Toynbee's A Study of History, Oxford University Press, New York and London, 1946, 2 vols. See volume 1, p. 115, for an insightful description of military brotherhoods.

23. In Landmarks of Homeric Study, the Right Hon. W. E. Gladstone proposes that Homer was a "nation-maker" and a "religion-maker" as well as a founder of the "rudiments of ethics" and of "politics." See pp. 56-88 for his interesting thoughts on Homer's religion. The book was originally published by Macmillan and Co. in 1890 but is out of print at present.

24. See Christopher Dawson's Medieval Essays, Image Books, Doubleday, Inc., N.Y., 1959, for his views on Southern French concepts of knighthood.

25. See Dodds' essay in Vlastos', the Doubleday Anchor Original, Modern Studies in Philosophy, Plato, II, Ethics, Politics, and Philosophy of Art and Religion, pp. 206-229.

26. In Dodds' phrase, "Greek rationalism" had "cross-fertilized" with "magico-religious ideas whose remoter origins belong to the Northern Shamanistic culture." (See p. 208, ibid.)

27. Again, Dodds emphasizes the "Orphic" nature of Plato's thought in his discussion of the "prolonged mental withdrawal" of Socrates, as described in the <u>Symposium</u>, 174d-175c. See p. 209, where he refers the reader to Festugiére's <u>Contemplation et vie Contemplative Chez Platon</u>, p. 69. Is this mental withdrawal visionary or simply meditative? Dodds argues that it is a special kind of discipline designed to modify the whole psychic structure" p. 209. This may miss an essential distinction between the rationalism of Greek philosophy and the meditative systems that are used so extensively in India. Greek philosophy is more "scientifc" and action oriented, while Indian meditation tends toward occult passive reception.

28. See the short essay on Indian brahmacharya (vow of celibacy) by Amiya in Christopher Isherwood's <u>Vedanta for Modern Man</u>, Mentor Books, 1951, pp. 303-304.

BIBLIOGRAPHY

Adam, J. , <u>The Republic of Plato</u>, 2 vols. , Cambridge, 1902

Adam,J. , and A. M. Adam, <u>Plato's Protagoras</u>, Cambridge, 1893

Adler, M.J., <u>Aristotle for Everybody</u>, Chicago University Press, 1980

Ast, D. Friedrich, <u>Lexicon Platonicum</u>, Berlin, Herman Barsdorf, 1962

Aristole, <u>Ethics</u>, Everyman's Library, Dutton, N.Y. , Translation by John
    Warrington, J. M. Dent & Sons, 1963

Atchity, John, <u>Homer's Iliad. The Shield of Memory</u>, Southern Illinois University
    Press, Carbondale, 1978

Austin, J. L. , <u>Sense and Sensibilia</u>, Notes by G. J. Warnock, Oxford, 1962

Bambrough, R., <u>New Essays in Plato and Aristotle</u>, Harper and Brothers, London,
    1965

Bertall R., <u>Kierkegaard Anthology</u>, Princeton, 1936

Blakeney, R. B. , Meister Eckhart, <u>A Modern Translation</u>, N.Y. , 1941

Campbell, Joseph, <u>The Hero With a Thousand Faces</u>, Bollingen Series XVII,
    Princeton, 1949

Cavendish, Richard, <u>King Arthur and the Grail</u>, Paladin, Granada Publishing,
    London, 1980

Collingwood, R. G. , <u>The Idea of Nature</u>, Oxford, 1945

Copleston, Frederick, S. J., <u>A History of Philosophy. Volume Three</u>, Image Books,
    Doubleday, Inc., 1985

Cornford, F. M. , <u>The Republic of Plato</u>, Oxford, N.Y., 1945 ,

Crombie, I . M. , Plato, <u>The Midwife's Apprentice</u>, London, 1964

Dawson, Christopher, <u>Medieval Essays</u>, Image Books, Doubleday, Inc. , N.Y.1959

Deutsch, Elliot, <u>Advaita Vedanta</u>, University Press of Hawaii, East-West Center
    Press, 1969

Dodds, E. R. , <u>Plato's Gorgias</u>, Oxford, 1959

Field, G. C., The <u>Philosophy of Plato</u>, Oxford, 1949

Fite, W., <u>The Platonic Legend</u>, New York, 1934

Friedländer, G. C., <u>The Philosophy of Plato</u>, Oxford, 1949

Friedländer, Paul, <u>Plato. An Introduction</u>, Bollingen Series LIX.1, Princeton, 1958

Fuller, B. A. G., <u>History of Greek Philosophy</u>, New York, 1923

Gladstone, W. E., <u>Landmarks of Homeric Study</u>, Macmillan, London, 1890

Gould, Thomas, <u>Platonic Love</u>, Greenwood Press, New York, 1963

Grube, G. M. A. , <u>Plato's Thought</u>, Haktett Pub., N.Y., 1964

Hackforth, R. , <u>Plato's Phaedrus</u>, Cambridge, 1952

Hamilton, W., Plato, <u>The Symposium</u>, Penguin Classics, 1951

Jaeger, W. , <u>Paideia</u>, Oxford, 1947

Knox, B. M. W., <u>Oedipus at Thebes</u>, New Haven, 1957

Levinson, R. B., <u>In Defense of Plato</u>, Cambridge, i953

Lewis, C. S. , <u>The Magician's Nephew</u>, Collier Books, MacMillan Inc. , N.Y. , 1955

Lindsay, A. D., <u>The Republic of Plato</u>, London, 1935

Mercade, Jean, <u>Eros Kalos</u>, Geneva, 1962

Moreau, J. , <u>La Construction de L'Idealism Platonicien</u>, Paris, 1939

Murdoch, Iris, <u>The Sovereignty of God</u>, London, 1970

Murphy, N. R. , <u>The Interpretation of Plato's Republic</u>, Oxford, 1951

Murray, A., <u>Five Stages of Greek Religion</u>, New York, 1955

North, Helen, <u>Sophrosyne</u>, Ithaca, 1966

Nygren, Anders, <u>Eros and Agape</u>, Harper Torchbook Ed. , N.Y. , 1969

Ollier, F., <u>Le Mirage Spartiate</u>, Paris, 1933

Otto, Walter, <u>The Homeric Gods</u>, Thames and Hudson, 1979

Plato, <u>Plato, Collected Dialogues</u>, Ed. Hamilton and Cairns, Bollingen Series
LXXXI, Princeton University Press, 1961 (Phaedo, Phaedrus, Laws)

Plato, <u>The Republic</u>, Crofts Classics, Translated by Raymond Larson, AHM
Publishing Corporation, Arlington Heights, IL, 1979

Plotinus, <u>The Enneads</u>, Tran. Stephen MacKenna, Faber and Faber, Pantheon
Books, Inc. , New York, N.Y.

Radhakreshnan, S., <u>Religion and Society</u>, George Allen and Unwin, Ltd., London,
1947.

Ramanan, K. Venkata, <u>Nagarjuna's Philosophy</u>, Samuel Weiser, Inc. , N.Y. , 1966

Renault, M. <u>The Last of the Wine</u>, New York, 1956

Ross, W. D., <u>Plato's Theory of Ideas</u>, Oxford, 1951

Ryle, Gilbert, <u>Plato's Progress</u>, Cambridge, 1966

Saraswati, Srimat Swami Shivananda, <u>Yoga Byayam for Students</u>, Nabajiban
Press, Calcutta, 1978

Scruton, Roger, <u>From Descartes to Wittgenstein</u>, Harper Colophon Books,
Harper and Row, N.Y. , 1981

Shankara, <u>The Vedanta Sutras of Badarayana</u>, Trans. George Thibeaut, 2
volumes, Dover, Inc. , 1962

Shorey, P. , <u>The Unity of Plato's Thought</u>, Chicago, 1903

Shorey, P. , <u>What Plato Said</u>, Chicago, 1933

Simmons, Joe, <u>The Warrior, Studies in the Sources of Spiritual Mastery, Sport
and Military Power</u>, University Press of America, Inc. , 1982
<u>Winning Wars, The Spiritual Dimension in Military Art</u>,
University Press of America, Inc., 1986

Singer, T. A. , <u>The Nature of Love, Volume I, Plato to Luther</u>, N.Y. , 1966

Stace, Walter, <u>Time and Eternity</u>, Princeton, 1952

Stcherbatsky, T., <u>Buddhist Logic</u>, Dover Publications, Inc. , New York, N.Y. , 1962

Taylor, A. E., <u>Plato, The Man and His Works</u>, Meridian Books, N.Y., 1957

Thompson George, <u>The Oreteia of Aeschylus</u>, Cambridge, 1938

Urwick, E. J., <u>The Platonic Quest</u>, Concord Grove Press, N.Y., 1983,

Versenyi, L., <u>Socratic Humanism</u>, New Haven, 1963

Vlastos, Gregory, <u>Plato, Metaphysics and Epistemology</u>, A Collection of Critical Essays, 2 volumes, Doubleday Anchor Original, N.Y., 1970

Vlastos, Gregory, <u>Platonic Studies</u>, Princeton University Press, 1981

Wilamowitz, U. V., <u>Platon</u>, Berlin/Frankfurt, 1919

Wild, John, <u>Plato's Enemies and the Theory of Natural Law</u>, Chicago, 1953

Wolin, Sheldon, <u>Politics and Vision</u>, Boston, 1960